Adapt

Melinda Brown

Copyright © 2021 Melinda Brown
All rights reserved
First Edition

PAGE PUBLISHING, INC.
Conneaut Lake, PA

First originally published by Page Publishing 2021

ISBN 978-1-6624-5585-8 (pbk)
ISBN 978-1-6624-5587-2 (digital)

Printed in the United States of America

To my daughter, Kimberley. Go live your dreams.

December 15

The overly sweet taste of the iced coffee in front of Hannah Marks was a welcoming sensation. The caffeine was an instant motivation for her to open her laptop and pull up her study material for the next exam in her class on immigration law. Her professor was a woman by the name of Lucia Abarra, with a thick Hispanic accent. A barrier for her at the beginning. A by-the-book kind of professor with little disregard for any type of excuses. Hannah performed moderately well in the course, with a grade point average of 3.4. The exam stressed her out, and the visit to the local coffee shop relaxed her. The patrons were mostly college students like herself, crunching down for their finals. Many of them were in small groups in the back, while others, like herself, were sitting solo. Pushing the strand of her wavy brown hair from her face, she navigated the computer's mouse to open up her notes she typed up from the last class session. Ms. Abarra outlined what chapters would be on the final. It was up to them to go back and reread to determine the necessary details to recall. Taking another sip of her coffee, she slipped on her wireless earbuds and brought up her phone's application to play some of her favorite songs. She needed to focus, and the shop's atmosphere of mixed conversations was beckoning her attention. She hoped that the exam would be something similar to the one she had that morning in her family law class. If only she were so lucky. Despite her past, that class she excelled in.

Legal matters subjected to family issues seemed to bother her. When she was fourteen, her mother decided to leave their home in Mastic, New York, to tend to her ailing mother in Wapakoneta, Ohio. A rural town with a population count laughable compared to New York City's. Her grandmother was the only grandparent still alive on her mother's side—a woman in her seventies at the time, with many medical complications, including a leaky heart valve. Hannah's mother, Delilah Marks, refused to place her in a home and didn't feel safe knowing that she was still living alone with no one around. Like Hannah, Delilah was an only child. The move to Ohio was supposed to be only temporary. That was six years ago. Two years into that, her grandmother passed away, but Delilah never returned to their house on Long Island. By that time, she and Hannah's father, Robert, became so apart that they grew out of love, or so Hannah believed. Holidays and visits were very awkward and less frequent as time passed. Her parents never officially divorced but were legally separated when she turned seventeen.

Her senior year in high school was the hardest. Her grades dropped slightly, and the idea of being accepted into New York University's prestigious law program was ho-hum. The motivation was lacking, and the excitement as any typical teenager should have had when stepping across the stage to receive their high school diploma was nonexistent. To her surprise, she overcame the funk she was in and continued her path, achieving good grades in her freshman year at NYU. Her choice of becoming a law student was hers alone, with inspiration from her father. He was part of a well-liked firm in Lower Manhattan that dealt with personal injuries. He made the daily commute of two hours to and forth to purchase their two-level home in Mastic County, New York, with the location just a few miles from Mastic Beach. Hannah still frequented her house on the weekends to head to the beach to catch up on time with her father and friends. Fridays were the best days of the week during her college semesters. She would take the subway down to her father's office to wait for him to leave early that afternoon. The two would commute together back to their house, stopping by the local Italian restaurant to pick up dinner. No matter how many times she frequented, it would be the same meal: baked spaghetti with two meatballs and a piece of garlic bread. She savored this meal.

Her phone chime prompted her attention, and she focused on her musings—an email message from her mother with the attached flight itinerary. Delilah scheduled her flight from Dayton, Ohio, to LaGuardia Airport on December 22. Two days after the beginning of her winter break from school. The message composition also contained a few sentences from her mother stating how excited she was to see her and learn more about her studies. Swiping the message quickly from her phone, Hannah sighed lightly, with a roll of her eyes. She blamed her mother for her parents' fallout. Her mother continually tried to salvage what was left of her daughter's relationship with phone calls, voice mails, texts, and emails. Hannah returned only half, claiming she was too busy to respond. In actuality, she just didn't want to deal with it anymore. It pained her to see her mother. A grim reminder of what her life used to be. Her father constantly encouraged her involvement with Delilah, and that often led to arguments. The visitations seemed forced. No hugs between her parents, only stiff handshakes or waves. A terrible plight for her winter break. One that she secretly wished for from her routine.

The final exam in immigration law ended around five that evening. An hour and a half. Longer than she planned. She struggled with a few of the essay questions and found herself second-guessing. She silently cursed her mother. The email was a distraction and reopened old wounds. Pulling her jacket across, she shivered as the cold air brushed lightly against her skin. Checking her phone, she didn't see any more messages that she missed, and turned the silent mode off. Feeling the laptop bag pressing up against her back, she embraced the chill and set off to stop by a local bagel shop to grab a quick dinner before retreating into her dorm to study for her final two exams scheduled for tomorrow. Halfway across campus, the sound of her familiar ringtone flagged her attention, and she took out her cell. "Hello?"

"Hey, sweetheart," her father spoke on the other end. "I meant to check in with you earlier. My day has been crazy."

"It's okay. I'm heading to grab some dinner. I think I did all right." She hesitated on how to respond with the uneasiness from her second test that day.

"I'm sure you did fine," he assured her. "I'm heading home from the office now. Did you get the email from Mom?"

"Yes." Her answer was short and curter than she intended. She grimaced inwardly.

Robert picked up on it. "Come on, Hannah…" he softly urged. The same argument ensued. "She's still your mother."

Sour, Hannah sighed hard on the phone. "I know, Dad. We had this talk before." She stopped to think about how her mother's email distracted her mind and could have cost her a passing grade on her exam. "What if I don't want her to be that anymore?" The words escaped her mouth quicker than her mind took the time to process. She herself was shocked by what she just plainly stated with affirmation. Was it indeed how she felt, or the stress exacerbation? The silence was the only thing she heard on the other end. No words. Guilt washed over her like a giant tsunami. "I'm sorry."

"It's okay," he finally broke the quietness. "I know you are under a lot. Look, we will attend the office party this weekend. I will introduce you to some of my partners. I know you would love the references for your internship program next year." He chuckled. "Not like you want to think about school over your holiday." A beat. "We will talk more about your mother when you get home. Deal?" Hannah didn't answer.

Fifteen minutes later, after cutting across the street, she reached the bagel shop: a small mom-and-pop business that was the talk of the campus. They specialized in gourmet bagels and soups. Their coffee was nothing spectacular. Three people were in the line in front of her, and she pulled out her phone to scroll through some of the day's social media posts to kill time. Background noise from a flat-screen television in the back grabbed her attention—a news alert. The female reporter's overly made-up face filled most of the screen before she stepped to the side to allow the camera to home in on the wreckage behind her. Traffic on a busy highway was at a standstill. A mangled tractor trailer blocked the view, and fire crew were putting out flames. A few patrons of the shop stopped their conversations abruptly to look on. "John, I have spoken to several witnesses who were on the scene and were fortunate enough not to be part of this deadly carnage. They all claimed that a semi lost control and flipped onto its side with its trailer protruding into the right eastbound lane. A car traveling in the same lane slammed into the trailer, and then a semi following hit it. Both the trailer, car, and second semi's cab caught on fire. The driver of the second semi was able to flee the cabin. However, the fire spread so rapidly and hot that the driver of the car is presumed dead since no one was able to get to them in time. All traffic on I-495 eastbound has been stopped, and all lanes are now closed. Traffic will be redirected. This will cause major congestion well into the night. The department of transportation is strongly urging everyone to take alternative routes."

The screen changed over to a male inside the reporting studio. He sat there as if he was waiting for his cue to continue the conversation. "Thank you, Olivia. What a terrible devastation to that driver and their family near the holidays. Keep us posted."

"Ma'am?" the bagel clerk called out to Hannah from the counter.

Blinking, she stood there stunned and looked at the clerk quizzically. She became so engrossed in the flash alert that she didn't realize that the other three customers already placed their orders and moved on. "Sorry." She fumbled for her student card. "Poppy seed tuna."

She was not very coherent that night when she awoke from the repetitive knocking on her dorm door. Groggy, she fumbled to grab her phone to glance at the time. Three in the morning. Along with notifications of a missed call and text from her mom. The only word from her mother was asking her to call her. She missed it two hours ago. Why would she call so late in the night? The room was still, and she could hear her roommate, Ashley, muttering from the top bunk from the intrusion. "Was that our room?" Hannah asked out in the darkness.

The knock again answered the question; this time, it was followed by a male voice. "Campus security."

"Shit!" Ashley jumped off the bed and grabbed her robe, quickly tying it around her. "I didn't do anything." The young blond woman looked over at Hannah.

"Hey!" Hannah snapped back defensively. Still half asleep. "Don't look at me."

Ashley beat the next knock and opened the door hesitantly. Hannah couldn't see the officer on the other end from her angle, though she could make out the conversation between the two. She overheard her name. Ashley turned questioningly to her roomie and opened the door wider to give the officer a complete view of their room. Standing up, Hannah looked the officer's way. "Hannah?" the older gentleman called to her. The authority in his voice was depleting. "Sorry to get you up this early. New York State Police is waiting in the office. They want to speak with you."

"The police?" Hannah cocked her head in confusion. She paused on obliging with the request. "What for?"

The campus security officer glanced slightly over at Ashley and then back at her. His eyes were betraying him. "I think it's best that you just come with me and talk with them," his words pleaded with her. The following five words shook her to her core. "It is about your father."

December 16

Hannah remained reticent in her plastic and metal chair as her mother sat on the left of her. Delilah Marks discussed the investigation's vigorous details into the fatal crash and the autopsy's handling with the sergeant across the large metal frame desk. The man appeared to be in his late fifties and of Asian descent. He was having her mother review various documents, thoroughly explaining each one. Dutifully, Delilah signed each one without hesitation. The mascara around her eyes ran some from the shed tears before the meeting with Sergeant Li. She managed to wipe away most, though some of the black was still there. Now she remained steadfast and tranquil. Crossing her arms, Hannah faded out. She wanted to get away from there. This was not happening! It was as if she was having an out-of-body experience or a nightmare that she watched from afar. She couldn't move or talk. She was trapped in her thoughts and feelings. Anger became her. Why was her mom so stable? How could she just sit there and sign away paperwork like it was a mundane event? This was about her father. Delilah's ex-husband! The father of her children! "Are we done?" Hannah barked, finally finding her voice. She glared at her mother with sheer resentment. She wanted to go home. Her dad was there waiting on her. She was sure of it. He was not dead! No way!

Her interruption caused Delilah to pause. The woman hesitated on her response and to look to Sergeant Li for assistance. The officer smiled warmly at her. "I apologize that this is very time-consuming. We want to do everything we can to handle this sensitive matter with you, miss."

That was not going to cut it! Snapping out of her chair, Hannah grabbed her purse and cellphone from the floor. "I'm going home. Dad is not dead! I don't care what the hell you tell me!" Hot tears flowed down her face, dampening her skin. Her body shook as she clutched her items tightly. "He's not dead!" Proudly holding up her cellphone, she quickly unlocked it and fired in his contact number with her fingertips. "You are mistaken!" She persisted as she listened in. One ring, and her dad's voice mail quickly picked up with his familiar greeting. Professional tone with the announcement of his title as an attorney in Manhattan. A proud achievement. Shaking her head feverishly, Hannah saw on the call log that she attempted the same number at least ten times within the same date.

Delilah finally stood up and reached out to her. "Hannah, honey…" Her voice cracked, seeing the pain in her daughter's eyes. "Please, I'm sorry, baby…"

Retracting away, Hannah held her phone tightly to her chest. "Go away! You never loved him!" Her accusatory tone was followed by her finger pointing toward the woman in front of her. "You left him, remember? You left us!" Racing the dial pad, she typed in the numbers again. He would pick up this time. She was sure of it! Seconds later, the same reaction. Straight to voice mail. This time, she let the message finish, and the beep follow. "Dad, it's Hannah. Look, I know you are busy and must be on the phone. That's why you are not answering…" She sobbed harder as her voice quaked. "Please… Dad, just call me back." Painfully ending the call, she dropped the cellphone and fell to her knees, seeking refuge on the floor, with her face buried in her hands. The tears flowed uncontrollably now as she could no longer contain the fear and anxiety that plagued her. As soon as she was on the floor, she felt her mom's warm arms drape around her to draw her close, and the sensation of her mother's breath against her face and hair, hearing her mother cry along with her. Her first reaction was to push off the hate she felt toward Delilah. Instead, she clutched onto her, burying her face against her upper shoulder area near the neck. Her world was falling around her. There was so much pain. She just wanted to end. Wherever her dad went, she wanted to be with him, even if it meant embracing darkness forever. She would welcome it. How could she go on without him? Despite her mother being right beside her during her grief, Hannah felt alone.

Waiting outside the sergeant's office, Hannah retreated there once she composed herself to allow her mother to finish up all the tedious paperwork. She pulled up her phone and scrolled casually through the day's posts. Not responding to any and not posting herself. She wasn't ready to face the world. How could anyone truly understand? Her father's name was not announced as the deceased, per the police. It would be up to her mother to permit that. They wanted to inform the next of kin first. That was her and Delilah. After what felt like an eternity, the door opened, and outstepped her mother with Sergeant Li. The man shook her mother's hand one final time, giving a comforting squeeze and a nodding gesture. His warm dark eyes panned over to where Hannah sat. A solemn smile on his face greeted her. "Miss Hannah, I am truly sorry for your loss." He pulled out a business card in his pocket and handed it to her. "If you ever need anything right now, you or your mother are more than welcome to contact me." Hannah accepted the card and quickly stuffed it in her pocket.

Wiping her eyes, Delilah smiled gently at the officer. "Will you notify the funeral home, Mr. Li?"

"We will in the morning, I assure you. Our autopsy report will come back once we compare the dental records. His death was very tragic, and I apologize that this is the only way to identify him." He left the rest of the meticulous details off purposefully to spare them of any gruesome images.

The somber car ride that evening toward their home in Mastic seemed to take longer than usual. Hannah kept her eyes out on the scenery as the vehicles' headlights struck her irises as they passed along the busy road. She ignored the grumbling in her stomach from the lack of food that day. "You want to pick up some dinner to take back to the house?" her mother suggested thoughtfully as she drove.

"No," Hannah shortly mumbled.

"You haven't eaten all day…," the woman pressed gently.

"No!" she growled. "Just leave me alone."

Delilah sighed hard, hearing the conflict from her daughter in the passenger seat beside her. "Come on, Hannah. It's just you and me now. We need to—"

This infuriated her. Hannah finally whipped her head around to glare at her. "You left a long time ago! It's just me now."

A relentless argument that raged on, a reminder of the turmoil in their relationship. Delilah shook her head side to side. "Let's not talk about this right now. Okay? Just forget it."

"Fine with me," Hannah agreed before turning her attention back toward the outside once again.

"Why don't you stay around the house tomorrow? Go through some things if you want," her mother spoke once again. "I'll head to the funeral home to make the final arrangements. I don't think you want to be part of that conversation. I can pick out a nice urn for him."

"How can you be so calm about this?" Hannah shouted to her, clenching her fists. "You are not cremating him! That's my damn father!" She sobbed hard, unable to hold on to the emotions that boiled to the surface once again.

Seeing her daughter upset once more, Delilah cringed and put on her turn signal to take the nearest exit ramp off from the interstate, pulling over to the median outside the lane and setting her flashers. Unbuckling her seatbelt, she leaned over and gently took her daughter to her once more. "I'm sorry, honey… It is painful to talk about this." She gently ran her fingers through the brown strands of hair. "I have to be strong. For you."

"I don't want him cremated…," Hannah choked on her words as she stumbled through her purse to find some tissues to wipe her face. "Not him."

"You heard what the sergeant said. It would be better this way. We don't need to see him the way he is now."

"Why didn't they get to him in time?" Hannah asked out loud as she wiped her tears. The tissue was not enough to dam up the flood that poured from her eyes. "Someone should have!" Anger and confusion intensified her emotions. She remembered Sergeant Li explaining that the fire's heat was sparked by the vehicle's fluids and gasoline, which prevented anyone from getting to her father's car. The car went up fast in flames. They would not be able to determine from the remains if her father passed away before the vehicle burnt up or not. He only gave hope to the former to prevent any pain that led up to his death. No good one should go that way—especially a loving father by the name of Robert Marks.

December 20

The hours ran together after the memorial service. Hannah remained reclusive in isolation in her bedroom, not wanting to be bothered by the outside world. Her bed's soft comfort and the overly sized teddy bear that her father won for her on Coney Island when she was a child remained tightly gripped in her arms. She desperately clutched onto it, hoping to catch a slight, faint hint of her father's scent on the plush material. In between the blur of hours, she would force herself to head down to the kitchen to grab something to eat. She was tactfully choosing times of the day when her mother was not around, or asleep. Empty packages of chips and crackers were scattered around her floor, along with bottles of water. Any other year, she would be in a jolly, festive mood. Baking sugar cookies to spread icing later with her father or watching some sappy heartstring-tugging movie about the Christmas spirit's endurance. Most of the films were about love. A novel idea, one that didn't grab her attention. She had a boyfriend now of five months. A steady relationship, if anyone wants to call it that. They went out from time to time, finding ways to meet in between classes or studies to grab some food or chat about their day. Greg was a junior at her school and often helped her with some of the classes since they had the same degree plan. He met her in the library when she was looking for an old article on microfiche. The two reminisced about professors and sort of hit it off. After a month of dating, they became physical, as society would have expected of someone around her age. She often spent the night in his apartment versus her dorm room. A small secret that she kept hidden from her father. Sex did not strike her as a serious step. Not like it was building them to marriage. She never really pondered on the idea of them falling happily in love after graduation. Not like those movies she watched while she visited her house in Mastic.

Her eyes watched the snowflakes begin to dance outside as they fell from the sky, picking up numbers within minutes. The outside looked cold and gray. The meteorologist earlier on the news report stated a 60 percent chance of snow reaching the tristate area, with precipitation levels reaching three to four inches. If this were any other time of her life, snow would have thrilled her. She always enjoyed being out in it, even when she grew up. If she were lucky enough to get some snow on weekends when she was home, she would often rush out of the house with her father to see if they could start a snowball fight. Another cold memory that sternly reminded her those days were long gone. The snow seemed to taunt her. Her father was gone. No more peeking into her room to tease her about beating her outside to start the fight. Burying her face against the back of the bear's head, she felt the soft material caress her skin gently. Her body ached as tears poured down her face once more, dripping down onto the bear's head. A chime on her phone indicated that someone was texting her. Sniffing, she turned away to look down where her phone was lying on the bed beside her, halfway charged.

The home screen displayed six unread text messages and two missed phone calls in the past two days. All from Greg. She disregarded the latest one like the rest. Uncaring to know the contents of the messages. He was at the funeral home, just like some of her classmates. He knew what she was dealing with. He told her he would give her time to grieve; why would he reach out to her so soon? This time, she made an extra effort to read the text. "Why are you not talking to me?" The question was accusatory. This irked her. A selfish, needy remark for sure. She just wanted to be left alone, to exist in her world with a population now of one. Greg was not part of that. Having a boyfriend did not interest her. A harsh notion. One that received no apologies from Hannah.

Everything happened so quickly. She was helpless to stop it. Her mother made the funeral home arrangements and then the memorial service took place a day ago, around ten in the morning. A brief visitation was held an hour before the service. Her father's urn on a table in the front. The centerpiece of the event. An iron-colored container with impressions of various seashells along the exterior. One that her mother boasted that she chose with her father in mind. This choice moved Hannah, and a sliver of her being tossed aside the veil of hatred that covered Delilah. Her mom and dad purchased the house when Hannah was only ten. Going to the beach on weekends during the summer was the highlight of each year. They would wake up early and collect seashells, playfully fighting over their favorites. Her dad used to leave trinkets around randomly in the house as a warm reminder of their next adventure. She still could recall some of their best times together for a woman who supposedly fell out of love with Robert, when he and she were the happiest, when Hannah was the most content.

Classmates who were still in the area and the professors came to express their condolences to her. An out-of-body experience for her. Everything was so surreal. She was there physically, thanking them with tearful smiles, though mentally, she was in the embrace of her father. She held onto him like a scared child who wakes up in the middle of the night from a horrific nightmare. She didn't want to be there. She was a hostage by society to be present. In the eyes of those who came, Greg was one of those visitors. He stood by her side, purposefully making a place beside her during the service, holding her hand, giving light squeezes now and then. Her eyes dared not to meet his, nor did she respond to his small tokens of affection. Like a zombie, she remained soulless and sat in the pew. The pastor spouted Bible scriptures and remarks of memories of her father given to Hannah and her mother beforehand. A few colleagues of the firm, including one top partner, came up to the podium to speak about how professional Robert was and how proud he was to know that Hannah was following her father's footsteps into the legal profession. He promised he would leave an open spot for her at his practice once she completed her schooling. A wide smile moved over to her from her mother, who sat beside her after hearing the declaration. An empty promise, Hannah assumed. She didn't know where she would be in her current mindset in the next few weeks or months. There was no desire to return to NYU to continue her studies. She wanted to fade away like the sunset into the night.

The reading of the will followed that afternoon. No pause to shed a tear. The lawyer advised that of the various life insurance policies and mutual funds, Hannah would receive five thousand to spend as she pleased, and the rest set aside in a mutual fund to pay for the remainder of Hannah's pregrad and postgrad studies. That included her room and board. Once she completed her schooling, the rest to be withdrawn in small increments to avoid tax penalties. Delilah would receive fifteen thousand. This shocked Hannah. Why would her father bother to leave her anything?

A timid rap at the door made her cringe and squeeze her bear tighter within her fingertips. The door slowly creaked open for the visitor. "Hannah, honey. You haven't come out of here in days…" her mother stated gingerly. "I would love to spend time with you while I'm still here…" Hannah refused to answer nor turn to look her way, keeping her back straight at the door. Seconds later, she could feel the mattress shifting downward slightly as her mother took the empty seat on the side behind her. A warm, gentle hand caressed the top of her back slowly. "You don't need to face this alone."

"I want to," Hannah broke her silence with resilience as she shunned away. "You left a long time ago."

At first, the older woman didn't answer, almost tempting Hannah to turn in her direction. "I want to be part of your life, honey. I always did."

"Yet you are leaving again." She leaned up to look more in her mother's direction.

"I wanted to talk to you about that…" Delilah left the remainder floating in the air for interpretation. Hannah never noticed until now, this up close with her mother, that age was taking over. The once-dirty-blond strands of hair were mixed in with several white ones, particularly on the upper roots. The skin around her face was sagging and no longer had the firmness as youth once brought. The prominent blue of her eyes faded to a lighter shade, like plastic items out in the sun over time. "Why don't you take next semester off?" Her words were suggestive of hope. Words that Hannah almost played into until she continued, "You can come back to Ohio with me and stay awhile." A slight smile formed on her face. "I bet it's been well over ten years since you were there last. Mom missed you."

Hannah snubbed her nose at the mere idea. "I hate Ohio. I hate everything about that fucking place," she hissed loathingly.

"Come on, Hannah—" her mother pleaded.

A familiar chime from Hannah's cell interrupted their dialogue and withdrew her attention downward. Another relentless text from Greg, now entirely demanding some sort of reply from her. She rolled her eyes. Why couldn't everyone just leave her alone? Delilah picked up on the unspoken expression from her daughter's troubled face. "Why don't you just text him back? I'm sure he would understand…" She paused thoughtfully. "Was he the one that sat with us during the service? He seemed like a nice kid."

"Kid?" Hannah scoffed at the description as she sat up straighter in her seat, possessively pulling the phone closer to her. "I'm not a teenager anymore, okay? I would just prefer you to stay out of my damn relationships too."

Cupping her face from the physical and mental exhaustion, Delilah ran her fingers through the top strands of her hair. Hannah's resentment toward her was wearing her down. "You can't stay here forever, honey… at least not in this house…"

"Why not?"

"This house is not paid for. Even with what I can get from the insurance policy, it wouldn't be enough to pay on the mortgage to keep you here."

"I'm not leaving here!" Hannah raised her voice in defense as she gripped the bedsheets underneath her as if she was physically going to be forced out.

"You can still attend college, sweetheart. Your dad's fund will make sure you can maintain your stay on campus. You could always fly and visit me on breaks."

"Or you could just sell your house in Ohio and come back here where we belong?" Hannah countered harshly. "I thought you liked living here. With me…" The words in her mouth choked her.

"Baby girl…" Delilah leaned in closer to scoop her up in a mother's embrace once more. Hannah moved away slightly to give a hint. Her mom pulled back in an awkward motion. "Moving is not the issue. I just couldn't find a job to make the kind of money that your dad was putting out to keep us here."

"You haven't even tried!" Hannah pressed on firmly, not letting up on her point.

Defeated, her mom slowly rose from the bed to retreat down to the first level of the house, where she stayed most of the time. No other words came from her. Hannah sadly followed her leave with her eyes as she pulled her knees up to her chest. Leaning her face down onto the bony ends of her knees, she sobbed once more. She hated the predicament she was placed in. The sought-out emptiness of her room led her back to her thoughts. Back to simpler times when her dad was still alive. Back to that terrible day and to the conversation she had with him before. Their subject was about the holidays and her mother coming in. Hannah openly expressed her dissatisfaction about the repetitive routine.

Robert pleaded with her to have a change of heart. To make things easier during the holidays not since they would all occupy the same house but because Delilah was her mother. He never spoke ill of the woman he was once married to, and after their separation, he never expressed a desire to turn to another to fill that void. It must have been hard on him as well. Hannah always believed that Delilah was the one who instigated the separation after deciding to stay in Ohio longer with her ill mother. In fact, after hearing her father's words of an urgent plea, was it a premonition of what was to come? A foreshadow of his death? The same argument ensued around the same time of year whenever her mother came to visit. When Hannah was younger, she purposefully took trips with her friends that overlapped the exact dates to avoid seeing her. This year, there was an ominous tone in his voice when she came to think about it. Was someone else speaking to her through him? Like a higher power?

Hannah was never the religious type. One trait that she inherited from her mother. Her dad, on the other hand, grew up Catholic and sort of kept the same traditions. Not a devout Catholic.

Guilt washed over like a giant flood as new emotions rocked her. Anxiety? Angst? Fear? She no longer craved isolation. Pushing her legs out over the bed edge first onto the smooth hardwood, she crept down the stairs to where her mother was. Taking each step in stride till she finally reached her destination at the bottom. Her mother was sitting at the kitchen table, with the day's newspaper scattered about in front of her. Delilah had her hands on the sides of her head as she just peered down whatever article was leering up at her. "Mom?" Hannah's mouth felt dry as she called out. It felt so alien to reach out to her.

The sudden talk sort of stunned Delilah as well. She stared back at her daughter with newly runny mascara down her face and red eyes. She had been sobbing to herself. Hannah frowned at her appearance. Did she truly break her? "Yes?" her mother's voice quaked.

"Want to grab some coffee together?"

December 23

The greeting kiss that Greg gave Hannah at her front door felt awkward as if she forced herself to return it with affection. A part of her didn't want him there. However, she agreed that she acted selfishly in ignoring his acts of concern by the numerous unread texts and missed phone calls. She invited him over that crisp morning, with the encouragement of her mother. The young man in his midtwenties scooped Hannah into his arms after they broke lips, and she could smell the pungent, expensive cologne that he constantly wore along his neckline. One of the lures he offered, among other things. His charming features included a trimmed black short-hair mustache and beard. Along with matching black hair on the top of his head, held firmly by styling gel to create tiny spikes all around. His body derived of smooth olive-colored skin from his Italian descent.

Gregory Agosti was one of the top achievers in his class, with an outstanding mock criminal defense trial that he took part in last October. Seeing him up there, addressing the jury with his opening arguments, amazed Hannah. He was so calm and collected. His professor chose him to be the defense attorney for a man accused of theft and arson. Hannah was not part of the jury but instead in the audience, persuaded from her seat. Not only did he steal the show that night; his captivation won her over, and amid their celebration that night at his place, she gave herself to him. He pressed the issue for weeks before; however, she was hesitant to jump right into bed with someone. After that night, she found herself staying at his place more and more instead of in her dorm room. She never told her dad or mother about Greg. She was not ready to have that conversation with them since after all, in their eyes, especially her father's, she was still their "little girl."

Moving to the couch in the living room, Greg took the seat right to the left of her, clasping her hand with his, squeezing gently. "How are you holding up, Hannah?"

"It's a struggle… I miss him." She lowered her eyes as her mind flashed to her father. He should be there in the living room with her on the day before Christmas Eve, not Greg.

Nodding his head in appreciation, Greg lifted her hand and slowly placed his lips on the backside tenderly. His brown eyes were staring at her as he performed the act. "You will get through it." His eyes lingered longer on hers more than she liked. There was something about them. A glimmer in them that was not amiss. One that she had seen from time to time at his place. The thought disgusted her. Did he perceive this as a chance to catch up on old times? Reclusively, she retracted her hand from his and held it in her lap with her other hand. His attempts to mourn with her seemed indolent. The meeting at her house served another purpose for him. The vile thought sparked anger deep within her. Guarded, she decided not to let on what she predetermined, wondering if her forewarning of him was a terrible misconception. "You are strong, baby. You will get through this." His eyes floated around the room that they were in, taking in the decor. "This house is burdensome to you." He patted her leg gently. "Don't worry, the trip to my parents' home tomorrow on Staten Island will do you good. You should get away from here."

Hannah cringed by the remembrance of plans they made weeks ago for their winter break from school. She was going to speak with her father about Greg and then meet up with his family on Christmas Eve morning. Her boyfriend seemed ready to take the next step to make their relationship more serious. An intellectual, beautiful woman in the legal field, the designation was a complete match for Agosti. In all her years growing up in the metropolitan area, she never ventured out to Staten Island. She heard about the ferry that you could take to get there, and the notion of having this opportunity did excite her. The original plan was to meet the family for an early brunch before heading back home in the evening to spend time with her father. Things changed drastically, and the event slipped her mind. She met the reminder with resistance. Shaking her head slowly, she frowned. "I'm sorry, Greg. I can't do it."

The cancellation made the olive-skinned man sitting next to her tense up as his jaw clenched. "What? Come on, Hannah. You need this, and my family already made plans…" he pressed.

"No," she shot back curtly, agitated that he would even try something like that right now. "I told you that I could not do it."

"Why not?" It took every being in him not to express his anger truly. She could tell it in the furrowing of his brow. Greg was biting his tongue.

"I can't leave Mom like this. Of all the days…" Her answer was neutral. A part of her didn't care how angry he was. She was grieving. Her mother was suffering. She felt the need to reconcile her bond with her mother now more than ever. Her dedication had to remain steadfast. Her boyfriend, on the other hand, failed to understand this.

Shaking his head in disappointment, he quickly stood up from the couch, turning to look down at her. "I can't believe this, Hannah." He was unable to withhold his emotions. "You are ditching me over a woman who left your life years ago. You told me yourself! What are we now?" He didn't give her the time to answer his question; instead, he quickly added, "I thought I was ready to take the next step in this. Are you? You need to do something on your part as well."

Hannah's mouth gaped as she stared blankly up at him. She couldn't believe what she was hearing. His inconsideration frustrated her to the point where she was indifferent about their relationship. Did she want him to walk out of that door, never to return? She held back the words that came to her tongue. "She's still my mother, Greg!" she snapped defensively. "You don't know the story."

"You told me that she left you to some damn redneck town in Ohio!" he matched the elevated tone of her voice.

"To take care of my grandmother!" Hot tears filled her eyes, and she suppressed the need to let them flow. She had to be strong. "My mom and dad broke up, but she still tried. It was me who pushed her away," she finally admitted it to him and herself. A revelation. After all these years, she finally realized that it was never her mother who isolated herself from them. It was Hannah's anger. Her mom and dad never spoke ill toward one another in front of her, so she never knew why things felt the way they did. Robert never once came forward and placed sole blame on her mother. Hannah just assumed that Delilah was the one who called the shots. Maybe she was wrong?

Greg scoffed at her. "You seem to like doing that to people, don't you?" Choosing to use her own words against her. The final straw. Hannah cracked, and she cupped her hands over her face as she cried. Why was everything go so wrong? She didn't plan on the day's meeting leading up to a breakup with her boyfriend. Not like she needed this right now, but it seemed like it was going in that direction. The man in front of her became quiet, and all she could hear were her desperate sobs. Seconds later, she could feel the cushion next to her squish down by weight as Greg took his seat once more. His arms reached out, holding her to him as he gently stroked her hair. "I'm sorry, baby girl," his voice softer, almost a whisper, as he comforted her. "I'm sorry. I shouldn't be doing this to you. Look, let's compromise? I'll cut the meeting short tomorrow. I'll have you back by the afternoon. Plenty of time with your mom." Hannah wasn't budging. She shook her head once again in disagreement. Her decision seemed absolute.

"I'm trying to be understanding of your situation, Hannah," Greg began.

She quickly cut him off, "You could never understand."

"Well, I'm trying to." He threw his hands up in the air in exasperation. "If we want a relationship together, then we both need to be in it. You need to give a little. I have been trying to be patient." He paused, then muttered under his breath, "Too patient if you ask me. All you have been doing is blowing me off."

Hannah stared at the man in front of her incredulously. She saw right through him as if he was nonexistent in her life. Maybe that was her answer and his. He read into the blank stare as silence basked in the room. "Are you breaking up with me?" he angrily accused. "Is that it?"

The situation was overwhelming, and she could feel the entire weight of the world on her shoulders, crushing her relentlessly. Her endurance was more elastic than she presumed. "No," she softly answered. "Right now, I just wish to be alone. Greg…" She hesitated on how much to disclose to him at the present moment, given the conversation's intensity. No time was probably the right time for what she was about to say. "Greg," she continued, finding her strength to proceed, "I'm taking a break from school. Mom's selling the house, and I'm going to stay with her in Ohio until next semester. She can't afford the mortgage."

"What about all that money your dad left you?"

"Most of it went to my tuition and grad school. I just…" She broke the direct contact with his gaze. "I just need to get away… from all this…" Tears of pain came to her ducts again. She fluttered her eyelashes to try to hold them back. "I need to fix what I lost with Mom. Dad would have wanted this." The proclamation brought a wave of inner peace to her soul. She almost felt released after the admittance. A small smile of gratitude formed on her lips.

Her boyfriend gaped at her in shock as he scoffed at the announcements. "I can't believe this shit." His frustration was boiling over into anger. "What about us? What about our relationship!" His tone was rising once again.

"I can still call you, Greg. You know that," she urged gently. "It will just be for one semester. Besides, you will be engrossed in your internship with that firm in SoHo. I would only be a distraction." Switching the focus from her needs to his own to help him cope with her decision. Taking his arm, she cooed, "There's an airport in Dayton. You could fly in during break?" Placing a tender kiss on his cheek, trying her best to reconcile what they had.

Greg was not moved by her suggestion and harshly pulled away from her. "Why would I go out there?" he ridiculed the notion. "To plant corn?"

"They do have a lot of cornfields in Wapak. I saw many when I was there as a kid. That's the only thing I remember." She giggled at her private memory recall.

He was unmoved and rolled his eyes. "Wapak? Listen to yourself, Hannah. Don't be like that. Even you said it was a hole in the wall." He took her hands once more in his and leaned in to kiss her gently. "Do me a favor. You go out there and then you fly here to visit. Deal?" His brown eyes were looking into hers as he waited for her reply.

"Deal." She leaned up and gently took her lips with his, kissing him sweetly. She was relieved that the conversation ended the way it did.

"When are you leaving?" he asked after they broke their lock.

"On the thirtieth. We will start packing what we can after Christmas." She panned her eyes around to everything in the room: the little knickknacks, pictures on the wall, decor, furniture. Everything was placed and unmoved since her father's passing. She frowned. It was hard to let go, even of the tiniest item in the room. She didn't want to lose her memories of him. She wanted to recall every loving moment she shared with him in the house. The idea of strangers staying there scared her. Trespassers.

Greg followed her gaze and brought her focus back to him, with his fingertips tenderly moving her chin. "We can make it work, Hannah," he said encouragingly, with a warm smile. "That's if you still want to be with me."

"Of course I do, Greg."

"Good." He kissed her again softly. "You can stay with me during visits. Just come back to me."

"You know I will," she said in between the kisses they shared on her couch.

"You know you will miss New York."

December 30

Desolate farmland, far as the horizon, was all that Hannah saw from her mom's passenger window as they made their way back to Delilah's house. A two-lane road was outside the home, with parking on the side available, making the stretch even narrower. The driveway was all gravel, and she could hear the gravel crunching as the vehicle's weight pressed down on them. The site lacked fanfare. In front was a seriously outdated white home about one-third the size of her home on Long Island. Its aged exterior had her guess it was built in the 1980s. It desperately needed a fresh coat of paint on the vinyl, and one of the black shutters that faced the road seemed a bit loose. Two giant concrete steps led up to the porch from the tiny sidewalk that ran parallel to the street. Two uncomfortable metal chairs with faded pillow seats sat at the porch entrance. The small flower bed to the front's left side was dormant, and an empty hanging basket rested on the porch off to the far side. Getting out of the car, she cast her gaze over to the neighboring houses. All were around the same type, with one having a window unit for air-conditioning. Was this mess the same house she used to play in during her grandmother's visits when she was a child? She cocked an eyebrow across the vehicle's top to her mother, who was standing still to allow her daughter to take the new change of scenery all in. The graying-hair woman's face was plastered with guilt and shame. "It looks kind of rough with winter," she explained as she motioned Hannah to follow her up the steps toward the house's front door, holding her keys. "Let me show you the inside and then we can come back and get our stuff."

The entranceway revealed a small living room with wood paneling on the walls, causing the room lighting to appear dark even with the two-floor lamps. A small comfy couch greeted them, with a fifty-inch television set on a stand directly across, near the front exterior wall. An outdated beige carpet spread throughout the floor plan into the other rooms. To their left, ahead, was the doorway that revealed a quaint kitchen with laminate flooring and floral wallpaper. To their right was a dark hallway that must have led to the bedrooms. "Wonderful," Hannah huffed under her breath as she scrunched her nose up at the sight, appalled. This place was a hole in the wall! She desired her open well-lit home on Long Island desperately.

Delilah moved beside her to the hallway. "You can have Mom's bedroom." She then chuckled at a private moment, "She still has that bed you liked when you were a kid." As they moved along, the narrow hallway ended with two rooms on each side and a small bathroom that they passed. "We will have to share the bathroom. I'm sorry, Han." Her mother stopped at the dead end and motioned toward the left room. Skeptically, Hannah took her time before entering, almost afraid to see what else would be revealed to her. Flipping on the switch, she stopped to see a large antique metal bed with a rose color canopy that draped elegantly along the top and down the posts. "I'll get our things. Look around. Your grandma still had all her stuff out. I never moved it," her mom softly added before leaving her there alone.

A tiny sliver of memory came to light as Hannah moved toward the bed. It was a very comforting familiarity. She laughed lightly at the memories of her begging her grandma to sleep there during their visits so she could play pretend. Her grandmother never turned the request down. Hannah would often lay in the bed beside her grandma and gaze up at the canopy, often pretending to be a beautiful princess inside a castle in a faraway land. Several photo frames beckoned her attention placed on the dresser's various spots to the bed's right against the wall. Most were black-and-white photographs. One was of her grandmother and grandfather holding each other tight when they were married and still in their vibrant twenties. Their gushing, warm smiles were a true expression of the immense love they had for one another. Her grandfather passed away when she was around the age of six, from lung cancer. What memories she still had of him were very dissolved. It was hard for her to grasp the concept of death, and his continuous absences finally sank in when she was eight. It didn't bear down on her like her father's passing. Then again, the notion of coping with a parent's death was on a larger scale. Another photo frame was of her grandmother and her mom when her mother was around ten. It appeared to be at some carnival, and Delilah was proudly holding out a prized bear that she won. Hannah smiled warmly again at the moving image. The sensation of these precious tokens frozen in time was ineffable. She reached out and gingerly traced her fingertip down the side of the frame, feeling the wood. Her grandmother loved her daughter so much.

The last picture on the dresser was of Hannah when she graduated from the sixth grade. She was blossoming. Her big smile was showing off her braces with pink rubber bands, with a matching shirt. She had to be color-coordinated. Her hair was neatly pinned up in a bun—her decision, and one that her mother perfected early that morning before the school photos. Hannah giggled as she recalled sitting on her bed, with her mother standing behind her with a mouth full of bobby pins sticking out. She kept nagging Hannah to sit still as the hairdo continuously was lopsided. After five struggles, the bun was set, and Hannah dared not to move too fast to make it fall out until her photo was taken.

"I remember that day," Delilah chuckled at the doorway after returning from the car with a handle to a roller suitcase in one hand and her other hand holding onto the strap of a personal item bag. "I never proclaimed to be a stylist."

"I can't believe all the pictures, and Grandma kept this one." Hannah frowned at the braces again. "Didn't you send her another picture?"

"I sent one every year," her mother explained slightly defensively. Moving away from the photos, Hannah sat down on the bed's edge and looked at the dark-red wallpaper with white floral designs in rows. Delilah followed her gaze. "Mom sure loved her flowers," she chuckled. "She never wanted to change it."

"Wallpaper is outdated," Hannah groaned.

With a playful smile, Delilah sat down beside her and gently patted her right knee. "Well, with the money Robert gave me, I can use it to spruce up the place. You know, get it up to par with some of those houses on those shows." She shrugged thoughtfully. "Who knows. Once the house in New York sells, we can use that money to make it even better. It's a seller's market right now."

Hannah shook her head at her mother's afterthought in disbelief. Furious, she sprung out of bed, spinning on her heel to glare hard at her. "You're going to spend Dad's money on this?" She tossed her hands up in the air.

"Why not?" Delilah was taken aback by her outburst.

"Why?" Hannah mocked her question angrily. "Because I would gladly settle for a house in New Jersey than this hicktown! I thought you wanted to rebuild what we had, not snatch me here!" She abruptly stopped herself when she saw the tears swell in her mother's eyes. The woman in front of her torn, facing an invisible battle. Seconds ago, they were reminiscing about the love they shared toward her grandmother. The previous owner of the home. The person she enjoyed visiting as a child and at the same place. She knew that things changed and people changed as they grew older. Her mother was holding on to those faded memories just as she was holding on to whatever was left back on Long Island. Guilt washed over like a dark wave. "I'm sorry," she sighed hard in defeat.

Shaking her head to dismiss the apology, Delilah rose from the bed's edge and wiped the tears at the cusp of her eyes. "It's been a long day with the flight and drive from Dayton."

"I agree." Hannah nodded her head with a soft grin. "Car rides over twenty minutes were never good to me. Get some coffee?" Her mind flashed to places of her usual hot spots on the island, such as the nearest big chain store five minutes from her house.

"That sounds nice. There's a diner up the road about two miles. They have some coffee you can get and maybe some food. I'm starving." Delilah moved the luggage onto the bed. "We can unpack once we get back."

The suggestion was nowhere close to what she was thinking. She scrunched her nose at the terminology placed before her. "Diner?"

December 31

The faint sound of a rooster cawing stirred Hannah out of her slumber. The animal's beckoning was unfamiliar, and she remained motionless in her bed, listening closely to see if her ears were deceiving her. As if on cue, the rooster cawed again. Groaning, Hannah rolled over onto her side and stared out through the transparent rose-colored curtains to see the pink sky as dawn was transitioning to the morning hours. "Fitting." She yawned with a grumble. Besides the bird, the outside was pretty calm. Unlike the sounds she was accustomed to on Long Island: cars driving out of her neighborhood to begin their commute to work, buses off in the distance to pick up their passengers to head into the city. She yearned for a busy life.

  Hearing her mom already awake in the room down the hall, she swung her legs out of bed first and rose on her feet, then reached over to her nightstand to pick her cellphone off the charger. No missed calls or texts. Cringing, she realized that she never reached out to Greg once she arrived in Ohio, and it was too early to call him now. "Fantastic," she sighed at her own mistake before heading off to the bathroom to refresh herself. Once reaching the hallway, she paused when she saw her mother's face poke out through the doorway and down in her direction with a warm smile. Her mother was always the morning person in their family, unlike Robert and Hannah. "Hey, hun. Did you sleep well?" she called to her, drowning out the radio in the bedroom.

"You mean besides the rooster waking me?" Hannah muttered.

A lopsided grin on Delilah's face was the response to that. "You will adjust. It's peaceful here."

"Deserted," Hannah corrected her.

Her mother was unmoved by her remark. The grin remained on her face. "I need to run into the office for a bit this morning to catch up on some things. If you drop me off, you can take the car and go explore the little shops downtown." Her announcement about the day's plans was a complete disappointment to her daughter. She could tell immediately by the frustrated look on the young woman's face. "Just for a few hours."

Hannah was not amused. She continued toward the bathroom and slammed the door, letting her anger be known. Her entire body shook as her emotions took off like a roller coaster. She couldn't hold back the tears that formed in her eyes. The two days were a grim reminder that life forced her to move on and accept the change despite the pain and loss that she endured. To "adjust," as her mother called it. Adjust to the fact that her father was no longer in her life. To leave all that she knew in New York to live in a small town that didn't seem very inspiring to anyone her age. To adjust to the idea that her mother would have to go on with her everyday life of working a full-time job while Hannah would have to be alone during the day. The concept of paying bills to survive was not foreign to Hannah. Her father worked hard. Still, she needed her mother right now. She required that bond. She felt so alone, like a tiny child alone in the dark. Sniffing to regain her composure, she eyed the bathroom door to see if her mother was waiting for her on the other side to change her plans somehow. To admit she was wrong in returning to work right now. Instead, there was silence. Reaching for her cell that she brought along with her, she opened her contacts list and scrolled to find Greg. She needed to speak with him. The bars on her phone indicated that she didn't have good reception. It was barely past one bar. The call wouldn't connect. "What the hell else is going to happen to me?"

A few minutes later, Hannah walked out to head back to her room to change and saw her mother sitting down on the couch in the living room. The older woman's conflicted eyes gazed upon her, expecting her to speak first. "I forgot to call Greg last night," Hannah blurted out unexpectedly. Probably not the words that her mother wanted to hear. What else could she say? "There are no bars here."

"Not the best area. I know," Delilah admitted. "When you get down to my office, it picks up better. Drop me off, and you can call Greg." She didn't address anything else. Defeated, Hannah moved back to her room to finish up getting dressed. Maybe having time alone would help her cope. Shopping did seem to always cheer her up. She and her friends would always hit the fashion boutiques in SoHo during her weekend trips and come back with her arms full of new outfits in style. A pair of jeans and a few shirts were just the cure she needed.

Forty-five minutes later, her mother pulled into her business's parking lot near a small-looking brick building that looked even smaller than Delilah's house! "Smith Agency" was displayed on a metal sign near the door, along with a matching taller sign near the front, out by the street landscaped with bare flowers that were dormant during the winter season. It was beginning to flurry as the tiny flakes rested calmly on the small SUV's windshield. Delilah reached over to her center console and began to swipe the eight-inch LCD screen to navigate to the vehicle's GPS. "I'm going to put in the Sunflower Café's address. That's right downtown. The shops are along the same street." Delilah opened the door and paused to look back at her daughter in the front passenger seat. The outside's cold chill outside made Hannah shiver as it worked its way inside the cabin. Passing off an encouraging smile, Delilah leaned over and gently kissed her daughter on the top of her forehead. "Two hours, I promise." Her gentle eyes glimmered as she pulled away. Hannah nodded her head acceptingly. She braced the cold to switch over to the driver's side and pressed her back against the soft leathery seat as she settled into place. The GPS was idle, waiting for her to engage in the predetermined route that it calculated. Watching her mother walk inside, she placed the car in reverse as she eased out of the parking space to head to the cafe. Two hours was a short amount of time. She would make it work.

It took her about ten minutes to drive from her mom's work location to the Sunflower Café. It was between what looked like an antique shop and a hardware store. The road was only two lanes, with buildings attached that sat parallel with the main street. Cars parked parallel in spaces in front of the shops made the lanes even smaller. Hannah eyed a public parking lot near the block's end and put on her proper signal to turn in. Only a few cars were beginning to be covered by the snow that picked up slightly. The temperature was starting to drop below freezing, allowing the flurries to stick to the frosty metal. After parking, Hannah first reached out to her phone. She was accustomed to wintry weather with her past residence in New York. The cold never bothered her, nor snow. She just hated having to walk in it. A call to Greg was what she needed before she explored the various shops. Predisposed about finding parking, she didn't have the chance to notice what there was to offer. The welcoming sign of a ring on the other end brought her comfort already. The call was going through. The happiness slowly faded as the crew continued without any indication of an answer. Finally, it placed her in his voice mail. Assuming that he either was commuting to his class and lost his signal in the subway, or was already in class, she defeatedly left a quick message asking for a callback and letting him know that she arrived in Ohio safely. She ended the message with a quick reminder that she missed him.

 Taking a short sigh, she glanced outside to see the town's emptiness, with slight signs of life as a few cars passed down the street. Buttoning up her coat, she slipped on her soft, warm brown hat and pulled it snuggly over her ears. Grabbing her cross-body purse, she set out to kill some time before she had to pick up her mom, keeping her phone clutched tightly in her hand. She was hoping that Greg would get her message and call her back. Chatting up with him would not make her feel so alone. Turning the corner, she began to walk down the sidewalk to glance at the shops nearby. She spotted the antique store and noticed its double-sided, stand-up wooden sign displaying a welcoming message to its customers and informing them of a sale that was currently going on. To the left of that shop was a hardware store that was still opening up. A man was outside talking to another gentleman in front of the store. The closest one was heavier set, with a pair of overalls and a farmer's hat. He appeared to be in his mid-fifties. The other had on rugged jeans and a T-shirt, with a ball cap and tennis shoes. Hannah's eyes widened by their attire. "Seriously?" She scoffed to herself, stifling a giggle. She figured this town was rural compared to the Big Apple but didn't expect it to be that rural. Down the end of the sidewalk were two small circular metal tables with accompanying chairs. A cute painted sign dangled just above the doorway, with chains attached to the awning. A bright-yellow sunflower was the big giveaway. Just in front of it was a consignment shop with a Help Wanted sign in the window. The remaining offices were a closed lawyer's office and a service for taxes. Hannah gaped at her choices with resentment. "God, this is it?" At least the café was open. She would get something to drink and hope that time flew by faster.

A bell chimed as she entered the quaint café. Soft jazz music played over the intercom system, which invited her to walk deeper inside. Six small circular tables were spread around inside. Only two were occupied: one contained an elderly couple enjoying their morning coffee and biscuits, while the other had a male who seemed to be eating fast to head off to work. A chalkboard with brightly colored writing hung on the back wall above the counter to list all the menu items and their prices. A short, heavyset woman in her late forties operated the counter with a charming smile on her face. Her whitening blond hair was tied up neatly in a bun. "Welcome, sis. What can I get for you?"

The title threw Hannah off. She stumbled for her words. "Um." She scanned over the menu quickly. "Sis?" she blurted out curiously.

The woman's pleasant smile widened, picking up on Hannah's more Northern accent. "New to this area?"

"Sort of." Hannah still felt off, and she could feel the customers' eyes on her with interest. "My mom lives here. I'm just in town." Her eyes picked up on a familiar item that she was craving: bubble tea. The choice lightened her mood extensively. "I'll take a raspberry bubble tea and a poppy seed bagel with light cream cheese." Of all the things, she never expected a small-town café to have bubble tea.

Why didn't her mother tell her about it? Then again, did her mom know she loved the beverage? After all, they hardly stayed in contact off holidays—her fault.

The café owner nodded and dashed away to set to work on the order fulfillment while Hannah stood there, feeling more comfortable in her surroundings. Hanging around the cafe was ideal. "Is there a mall around here?" she called out to the woman as she was mixing her bubble tea near the register.

"Yeah, in Lima."

"Uh, where's that?"

"About thirty minutes away. They have some brand names there." The woman returned with her tea and fetched the bagel.

Hannah frowned at the response. Thirty minutes was not something she was expecting. Too long of a drive to get anything done. Maybe she and her mom could go there one day together. The idea stashed away in her mind to bring up later in the day. What a horrible place! No shops that appealed to her, and the closest mall was thirty minutes away. She glanced down at her cell, which was still tightly gripped in her hand—a lifeline of hope. Maybe Greg would call her soon?

Hannah arrived a few minutes early at her mother's place of business. The wipers removed a few flurries that remained on the windshield. Thankfully, the snow tapered off, and the accumulation was less than an inch. She could take one glance at her phone to see there were no return texts from Greg. Where was he? Paranoia crept inside her brain. What if he already found someone else? Long-distance relationships were complete struggles and failures to many. Despite leaving on good terms, their status was pretty unstable. Would he turn his back on her so rapidly, though? A knot formed in her stomach. A blur grabbed her attention, and she looked up to see her mother moving over to the passenger side of the vehicle. Her presence released the tension in her body and blocked any more negative thoughts on the situation. As soon as Delilah sat down, she glanced toward the back of the vehicle with a disappointed face. "You didn't buy anything?" she casually asked as she closed the door, shutting out the frosty air from outside. The ruffling of her coat was the only sound in the cabin beside the engine's idling.

"Didn't bother going in," Hannah replied, backing the vehicle out of the space to head back to their house.

"Oh?" The unspoken secondary question lingered in the air.

She grasped onto it and scrunched her nose at the suggestion. "Seriously, Mom? Antiquing?"

"You never know," Delilah softly suggested as she unzipped her coat, typing in her address for her daughter on the vehicle's onboard navigational console. "You could have hit the mall, I guess. I forgot to tell you about it."

"Yeah, the one thirty minutes away?" Hannah groaned. "Fucking can't stand this place."

"Hannah!" her mother curtly disciplined her. She shook her head in disappointment. "Language."

"I am a college student," Hannah argued, defending her use of the jargon, silently resisting to use more unsightly words. "I want to go back home. I can't stand it here. What the hell am I going to do for months?" Her emotions were breaking the invisible dam that she barricaded herself. "Sit around and drink bubble tea while you work?"

"Oh, you found the café." Her mother picked up on the acknowledgment. "They have good food there. I sometimes buy stuff for lunch from there."

Her daughter detected the diversion, and this made her roll her eyes. "Maybe Greg was right…" she muttered under her breath.

"About?"

"Just moving out here."

"Look, once the house sells, we will have to go back to clean it up and pack up more items," she assured her warmly. "We can make a week of it."

This did not amuse her. Hannah narrowed her eyes at the insult of a suggestion. "I may just end up staying there." The woman beside her could only sigh. She lost the battle for now.

For the rest of the day, Hannah isolated herself in her new bedroom, scrolling through social media posts on her phone and catching up on a few chapters of her latest novel. She didn't want to speak with her mother further. A gentle rap at the door around eight that evening caught her attention. "Hannah?" her mother's voice beckoned to her on the other end.

Sighing from the interruption, she answered, "Come in," not bothering to sit up from the bed to address her.

Delilah stepped in a few seconds later and stared across the room at her daughter, with a look mixed with worry and hope. "I made some popcorn. Extra buttery, just the way you like it."

The gesture didn't make her cringe. "I'm not hungry." Keeping her brown eyes glued to the lines of words in her book. She reread the same sentence at least four times as she pretended to be engorged.

"Come on, Han," her mother pleaded. "What better way to kick off a few days together than to start by watching a movie with a bowl of popcorn?"

The idea tempted her. Her early childhood days called her. She recalled sitting down on the couch on Saturday nights, snuggling up against her mom, watching a movie together. Typically, it was the same one over and over: a Hollywood fairy tale involving a young woman of royal stature following in love with a peasant boy that wasn't part of her class. The turmoil caused the castle's household and the journey that the two took together to escape society's wrath while facing sorcery and fierce creatures of one's imagination. The ending was like any classic. Good prevailed, and the two were able to maintain their relationship while everyone seemed to accept it, and lived happily ever after. Her mother was a helpless romantic, while her daughter was intrigued by all the knights, castles, and princesses. She never grew up from it, even if the movie was many years old. "I'm coming," she gave in as a peace offering to reconcile the disharmony between the pair that day. A temporary truce. It would take more than a movie and popcorn to merge the gap that time induced.

Settling down on the plush couch, she happily accepted the large bowl of popcorn and tossed a few of the kernels into her mouth. Her mouth was salivating at the salty taste after realizing that she skipped dinner that evening. Sitting down beside her, Delilah grinned and unpaused the DVD movie, having it play right at the opening credits. The title came across along with the familiar lute pluckings. Hannah's eyes became wide after instantly picking up on the tune. She looked at her mother in disbelief, holding the next kernel with her fingertips. Her silent look was begging for the affirmation that she sought. "I have it." Her mother grinned playfully. "Do you think I never enjoyed this movie? I saw it at the store just a few months after I moved here. I thought of you." Tears of joy seethed in her eyes, and Hannah quickly wiped them nonchalantly before popping in two more kernels. The words hung in the back of her throat. Her mom caught on with a warmhearted smile. "Hannah," she began gently. "You're my daughter. I never stopped loving you. I still cherish all of my memories. It's been lonely here without you." A beat. "And Robert."

Picking up on the unspoken hesitation, Hannah lifted her head at an angle to glance her way. "Did you stop loving Dad?" A question that resonated within her subconscious throughout her teenage years. Ever since that horrible day when her parents announced to her that their marriage was dissolving. Anger pushed sadness to the curb with the desire to denounce the woman in front of her. "Why did you abandon us?"

"I never abandoned you," Delilah shot up cautiously. "Mom was ill, and I was the only child. With your grandpa already passed, she had no one really with her."

"Don't they have homes for that?" Hannah pressed, rehashing old wounds. "I mean, you could have at least brought her to New York."

"Hannah, honey," her mother answered tolerantly. "This was her home. Besides, she was frail, and I don't think she could have made the trip. I guess." She sighed sadly. "I guess you never think about these things when you are younger. When I went to college long before I met your father, I never thought my parents would one day just pass on. I mean, it's inevitable..." She stopped abruptly and saw the troubled look on her daughter's face. Her husband's untimely death echoed in the air. Treading lightly, she continued, "I couldn't just leave her up here alone. Not when she needed me. It was a tough decision to make, Hannah. You were in high school. I guess

I assumed you could handle it. I just never thought the time away would drag on much longer than it did. Mom was in bad health for so long. Watching her suffer, I couldn't leave her side..." Her voice cracked as the painful memories hit home.

Hannah witnessed her mother's internal conflict and the sorrow that impaled her. She frowned as she listened in. She was listening for once in her life. Through the devastating years, she refused to do so. She cursed her mother loudly and cut off all communication. She blamed her mother for everything. Surprisingly, she graduated high school with top grades despite the turmoil. The school was a sanctuary for her. Away from the discord in her home. A welcome distraction. Reaching out, she took her mother's hand in hers and gave it a slight squeeze. "Mom, I love you..."

Stunned by the longing of her daughter's bond to reveal itself again, Delilah grew silent and clasped her daughter's soft fingers in her grasp. Returning the squeeze affectionately, she shook her head sadly. "I never meant to harm my marriage with Robert, nor lose you. After a year of me staying here with Mom, Robert became more distant than just the physical mileage. We started to talk to each other more as acquaintances rather than as an intimate couple. The sad thing is that we both agreed on that, and I never was hurt by it. Mom passed a few months after we decided on it, and I just remained up here."

"You could have worked on it again, Mom. It was never too late. I'm sure—" Hannah finally found her voice to rejoin the conversation.

"I wanted to... I guess I was too scared," she chuckled lightly. "When you get to my age, I guess romance is out the window."

Hannah tossed her a silly grin. "You are never too old, Mom." A huge weight seemed to lift off Hannah's shoulders. A cross that she bore for many years. Leaning over, she embraced her mom tightly and allowed the tears to stream down her cheeks, moistening her face. "I love you."

Delilah returned the hug and gently kissed her daughter on the forehead. "I love you too, sweetie. I want to make this work between us. At least I'm not too old to still be your mother. I know Robert wanted it."

"He did." Hannah laughed softly as she wiped the tears from her face. "He pushed me right before he died…"

"Then I'm sure he's smiling right down over us." Her mother patted her leg as she settled back down on her spot on the couch. "Trust me. This town is small. It took me quite the time to adapt to it."

"I don't think I can…"

"Give it a chance. You may make some of your best memories to come here."

This aroused a chuckle of amusement from Hannah. "In Wapakoneta? Yeah, right."

January 1

The familiarity of her surroundings eluded her in the mist that clouded her vision. Though the sad situation she found herself in was too recognizable and painful to forget. She was reliving the tragedy that occurred right before Christmas. The night of her father's untimely death. Her perception of the current state graced her with the knowledge that it was all a nightmare. She was sentient. However, her malicious subconscious continued to let the memory shards fall into place. She was home on Long Island. Darkness crept all around the windows as a telephone rang a few feet from her. The dreaded news of the accident that killed her father. She was restive. She dared not to pick up. A glimmer of hope that devastation was nothing more than a nightmare wrapped up within a nightmare. Her father was alive and well. She continued to whisper to herself. If she ignored the call, then his life would be spared. The rings continued, long beyond any normalcy. She would not yield! Yet the messenger continued to beckon her. The reaper. The harbinger of her father's death.

As the phone relentlessly rang, her mind began to stir to her conscious state. Now just on the layer of REM sleep. The ringing pleaded to her. It was then when her eyes snapped open that her cellphone beside her on her grandmother's nightstand was ringing. Groggy, she groaned from the feeling of lack of sleep as she rolled over to fumble for the phone, picking it up on the last ring. The caller's second attempt at a connection. "Hello?" Hannah sleepily answered. Her mind was not fully alert yet. She had no idea just what time of the morning it was. It felt like it was still pretty early.

"Hey, babe," Greg's recognizable voice replied on the other end. "Did I wake you?"

"No," Hannah lied with a resounding yawn. "I was getting up." Her face snuggling against her pillow as her body begged for five more minutes.

"Sorry that I didn't get back to you earlier. My day was crazy. I have to prep for two cases going to trial next month with my internship. Plus, Professor Miles decided to dump a workload on me with having to read five chapters by next week and write a quick essay on the case law."

Hannah nodded her head in admiration. Discussions of his classes always overwhelmed her and made her fearful of what would come to her. She knew in the end that the payout would be astonishing, and her father's firm would keep their commitment to finding her a position there once she received her diploma. It felt so far away. "Wow. It sounds like quite a mess."

"Yeah, one case is in criminal court. That's all I can say about it," he reminded her of the confidentiality agreement he had with the firm.

"Such a tease." She giggled lightly as she rolled onto her back to relax and stretch. The morning's sunshine rays were peeking through the window's glass and past the drawn curtains.

"You sounded rough when you answered. You doing okay, Hannah?" A tiny hint of concern draped off the question.

"Just a nightmare about Dad." She sighed sadly as her father's memory crept back into her mind.

He chuckled at her answer. "Figured you would have a hard time there in farm town. I told you to stay here."

"They do have a lot of cornfields," Hannah agreed with a slight chortle. "It's not too bad, I guess."

"Don't kid yourself," he disagreed sharply. "I know you hate it there. I know you miss me, and I miss you a lot."

"We can do a vid chat one day." She smiled softly at the assertion of his affection to her. A warmth overcame her like the rays of the sun beaming through her room and onto her bed.

"Not the same," he jeered. "I don't think I can make it another month and a half to wait for you." There was a slight pause in his statement, but not enough time for her to respond. "Another reason why I wanted to call you right away. I got some good news."

"Oh?" She gave in.

"In two weeks, I have a short day that Friday. I talked to my parents, and I thought if I could fly you in the afternoon, you could spend the whole weekend with me there at their place on Staten Island. You know, to make up for Christmas?" The latter part of his announcement was thrown at her like a dagger. Sharp and easy to cut her. "You could fly out Sunday midafternoon."

Hannah winced at the predetermined plans. She bit her lip as she mulled over it. She wasn't expecting this. If it were right after she arrived in Ohio, she would have jumped at the chance without any hesitation. Now she didn't know what choice to make. She and her mother were torn apart for many years. Their relationship wouldn't fix itself overnight with just a movie and popcorn. It would take time. A time that she wanted to devote herself. Any deviation from that path may set her back to square one. "Greg..." His name lingered at her tongue's tip.

Greg picked up on her unspoken words. An exaggerated sigh poured out of his mouth on the receiver. "Don't tell me that you want to stay there."

"I'm trying to spend time with Mom as we go through this," she softly reminded him.

"With the woman that was out of your life since you were a teenager?" His rebuttal was chastising.

It took every fiber in her being not to disconnect the call then and there. Hannah's body shook as her emotions soared. Not how she wanted to start her morning. The placement of pressure angered her, and she solely blamed him. "That's not fair, Greg!" her words harshly snapped at him.

"No, Hannah," his voice elevated in twine with hers, cutting her off abruptly before she could finish her defense statement. "You are unfair to me." Using her own words against her. "I have been patient while you dealt with everything. Fuck. Even more patient than most guys. You need to make this work with me."

Shaking her head in disbelief, she pulled the cell from her ear and glared at it as if she could see his face. Tears rolled, and she quickly wiped them away. Pressing the phone back against her ear, she heard him continue his aggressive posture, "You are still coming up on break, right? I mean, that's a done deal. Correct?" His persistent confirmation agonized over her. It was as if he was proceeding with a case against her, placing her on trial. This offended her. She refused to be his guinea pig. Not like this.

In hindsight, her plans with him to hang out during their break, as they discussed before her leaving New York, never really loomed in the air with everything going on. Plus, the date was so far away. She wanted to spit at the sheer mention of it now. However, she knew placing salt into the wound during their discord would not be wise. She may regret it. Though with him acting like an ass, she didn't think the notion was too far-fetched. She felt newfound strength resonating within her. "I will get back to you later this week after I see how things go." The open-ended acknowledgment was not what he was looking for, and she knew it. She answered the questions almost in a smug-like tone. More intentional than planned. She had no idea where her relationship would be with her mom at that point.

"Bullshit," Greg mocked. "Can't believe you are doing this... I need to know soon. Do you know? Make the flight plans." He sighed heavily again. "Come on, Hannah. We agreed on this. Why are you even doing this?" He didn't let up as he replied to his inquiry. "I should have seen this coming. I can't believe that you want to fucking stay there in the cornfields."

"I told you that I would get back to you, Greg." Hannah refused to let his antagonizing behavior play into her. "That's not a no."

"So? Is this what you want?" he shot back defensively. "To simply vid chat when you feel like it and just show up whenever you think it's right with your mom? The same mother you had nothing to do with until your father died. When will that be? Huh? Six months? A year?" He derided again at his thinking. "I'm not waiting around like this. Being jerked around. I'm tired of this shit."

His continuous cursing rubbed her the wrong way. It only bolstered her resolve. "What's that supposed to mean, Greg?" Turning the hostility back against him. She smiled knowingly. Two could play at this game.

"You know, Christina called me last night," he admitted. Upping the ante. "I didn't want to tell you because it was nothing."

Hannah knew the name well. Christina was Greg's ex. The two had a falling out about three months before Greg asked her out. She was in the same class year as Greg. Their breakup was a mystery. All he would disclose to her was that it was Christina's decision. He suspected she was cheating on him. At least that was the story he told her. Hannah now wondered if he was only spooning her to get her pity to accept his date request. "What did she want?" The roughness of her question revealed that he plucked a nerve.

"She wanted to get back together. She missed me, Hannah." He paused for a few seconds, allowing the reality of the situation to settle in. "I thought we were good, so I told her that I was still with you. I turned her down." He didn't let up. "She wanted me."

"Why didn't you?" Hannah felt the sadness wash over her like a tidal wave. Jealousy raved inside her.

"Because I thought we were together. I was trying to make it work. Now I feel like a fucking idiot. Maybe I should have gone back to her," he pressed, placing the ball back into her court.

Shaking angrily, Hannah took a slow deep breath as she closed her eyes. She felt so weak and powerless. She was stabbed in her already-fractured heart. "You're right, Greg. Let's just end it." She pressed the disconnect button on the cell, abruptly ending the call, getting in the last word. If he dared to call back, she would ignore his call. She knew she seriously pissed him off by doing what she just did. Right now, he would be fuming and hoping that she would see the error in her ways and come groveling back to him. No, she moved to Ohio for a reason. It was to rebuild her relationship with her mother. Too many things held her back. Her father wanted it to work. She owed it to him, even if it meant losing her boyfriend. A part of her agreed with his temperament of the matter. It was selfish of her to make him sit and wait for her to come to her senses. Perhaps the path she was taking did not include him. It felt that way. This relationship was not the first breakup she had in her life. She lived through three others ever since she turned sixteen. It probably wouldn't be the last either. Maybe fate told her she had to be alone. At least for now. Pulling her knees to her chest as she sat up in the bed, Hannah tossed the cell indifferently beside her as she cried. She allowed her body to open up to excommunicate all the feelings she had before—a purge.

A few minutes later, a soft knock came on her door. Wiping her eyes again, Hannah found the strength of her voice once more. "Come in."

The door slowly opened, and her mother timidly peeped around the edge. "Everything okay, sweetie?" A genuine look of concern surfaced on the older woman's face. "I heard your call in the next room… Well, at least for what you were saying… sounds like a rough call."

"Greg and I broke up…" Hannah admitted as she took a breath to try to calm herself.

"Hannah, sweetie." Her mother moved toward the bed to help her confide in her. She reached out and gently scooped her daughter in her arms as if she was a young child. Delilah held her gently in her embrace as her fingertips moved through the top of her hair. "Don't ruin your life because of me. You can go to New York and see him and your friends whenever you want. I know right now, this place is not where you want to be with your life. It took me a while to adapt to it. There are good people here. You don't have to sever ties with your friends though. I'll be here when you get back."

Hannah shook her head feverishly, resisting her old social networks' assurance and healing her rocky relationship with Greg. Though, at her present state, she wasn't even sure she wanted to go that far. "I lost Dad. I'm so afraid of losing you, Mom. I want to stay here. Try to make it work."

Delilah smiled at her warmly by the news. "I want to make it work too, honey." She kissed her daughter gently on the forehead. "For Robert's sake. We can get through this. I know it's rough with my work and all. I'll do my best for you."

Hannah leaned up with a gentle return of the smile. "Sounds great, Mom." Feeling proud to use that term again to address the woman holding her.

"How do you feel about some breakfast?"

January 9

The house was blistery cold that morning as Hannah's lavender plush slippers tapped the maple-colored hardwood flooring. She shivered despite the warmth of her flannel pajama bottoms with matching long-sleeve, button-up top. Her brown hair clipped off her neck. She could already hear her mother in the kitchen, brewing her morning's dark roast coffee. The air's aroma was a calming sensation that stimulated a smile to appear on her nude face. Her love of coffee was a trait that she indisputably inherited from her mother. At the door, the smile lingered as she saw Delilah humming gently to herself, pouring a bowl of cereal, her back to her daughter. Turning away, Delilah jumped when she saw her daughter in the same room, unannounced. To save face, she gave a playful smirk. "I got coffee on… and"—she moved swiftly to the fridge and pulled out a creamer bottle in delight—"got your favorite. Hazelnut."

"Are you trying to cosset me, Mom?" Hannah proceeded to sit down at the table to await her freshly poured cup of coffee.

"Hey, we girls need it from time to time," Delilah happily countered as she fixed them both a cup and sat down across with her.

Sipping gently on the hot beverage, Hannah sighed softly in slight ecstasy as the liquid's temperature created a warming sensation down her body, counteracting against the frigid temperature outside. A polar vortex and places that struck the region were well in the teens during the day and below zero at night. The house's heater constantly ran. "I needed this."

"Are you sleeping better?" her mother asked with deep concern. "I noticed you have been going to bed sooner than before."

"Yeah… slowly getting there," she admitted somberly. Silently still, hugging herself. The nightmares were not as frequent, and her mind graciously didn't think about Greg for the past three nights. The first days following their breakup were rough. She constantly had second thoughts about what she said to him, and a part of her wanted to reach her phone and dial him up. She tried to apologize for treating him and acknowledging that the person to blame was her. Yet a voice in the back of her mind made her resist. It kept her steadfast from going down that path. Her brown eyes looked her mother's way as she took another sip. "What did you want to do this week?" Fortunately, Delilah's boss was a fellow widower like her. A man in his sixties who lost his wife to breast cancer three years ago. He never remarried and still mourned her passing. They were married for fifty years. She made it that long. A promise she told him once she had her diagnosis one year before her death. The prognosis wasn't good, and she had underlying health conditions that would complicate the much-needed chemo treatment. She decided to withhold the treatment and live her life to the fullest until her passing. She accepted fate. She didn't want to be bogged down by the side effects of chemo and whatever else it did to her preexisting health conditions. She died peacefully in her home after hospice was called a month before her death. Her boss's friendly and happy demeanor never revealed the sadness in his heart, and one would not know that he was alone in this world unless they asked about it. He understood what it meant to be in pain. Without hesitation, he agreed to let Delilah have another week off to spend time with her daughter. He proposed it and stressed the importance of it. The workload could wait, and he even said he would help with the burden. Today was the first day of her mother's vacation. "What did you want to do?"

Delilah tossed a playful grin her way in response as she sat down her cup. "Want to do a home project?"

This stirred a giggle from Hannah. "Been watching those TV shows again.?"

"No, I'm serious." Her mother joined in on the good laugh. "I've meant to take down some of the wallpaper. I just haven't had time to do it."

The announcement was shocking to her. Not what Hannah expected at all. She knew how much the house's original appearance meant to her mother. "I thought you said you didn't want to change what Nanaw picked out." Calling her grandmother by the title that she used when she was a child. No matter her age, it never dropped out of her vocabulary. Her grandmother preferred it.

Delilah nodded her head. "I know, but like I told you, we all need to adapt to change." She sighed sadly. "The time has come. Besides, Mom would be happy to know that you are finally back at her house and sleeping over in her room again." Tossing a knowing smile her way.

Reaching over, Hannah gently clasped her mother's hand with hers, giving it a gentle, comforting squeeze. A talk that they never shared. She never grasped the reality of how hard Nanaw's death impacted her mother. Shortly after the funeral, she saw her mother, but the visit was short-lived, and Delilah put on a brave face. In hindsight, her mother was mourning alone. She was alone in Ohio, trying to do all the required paperwork regarding her mother's estate and financial orders. She was isolated from her family—their separate lives forcing seclusion. When Robert died, Delilah once again had to deal with the affairs. He still made her the executor of the estate despite their separation. The decision made when Hannah was underage. Robert never bothered to have it amended when she turned eighteen. After all, most people his age would not ponder too much on the concept of death. Hannah was near her, but still, Delilah was alone. Hannah shut her out. Anger and resentment were all that she saw toward her mother. Anger for the untimely death brought upon her father, and bitterness for her mother. She blamed her for everything—an unfair position. Looking back, Hannah knew she was in the wrong. "If you want to do this, Mom, I'll help."

"I do." Delilah regained her composure and inhaled as she returned the squeeze of the hand. "We can do the bathrooms first. I'll let you pick out the paint for one of them. There's a local hardware store in town. We can go there."

"Sounds like a plan."

The trip to the hardware store was felicitous as Hannah shopped with her mother. Their cart was full of plastic bags containing rollers, pans, brushes, stirring sticks, and two gallons of paint. Delilah let Hannah choose the color. The sample chart labeled the selected type "Hopeful," with a matte finish. The offspring of mauve and salmon. The name called to Hannah as if it represented a double meaning, especially when she wanted it to be her bathroom tone. Her grandmother loved the shades of pink, so she wanted something along those lines in remembrance of her. It was as if her grandmother's soul was calling her.

The same plea her father gave to her on the night of his passing. So far, the bonding with her mother seemed to be going a lot smoother despite their rocky start. The sound of a loud diesel engine caught Hannah's attention as she pushed the cart down the aisle in the direction of her mom's car. A dark-gray lifted truck pulled into the space behind their vehicle. Dings and rust were in various places. A work vehicle. She had no idea what year nor what model. A man in his late twenties with sandy-blond hair was in the driver's seat. She noticed his sideways glance as he turned off the truck and slipped on a black ball cap. Shifting her eyes rapidly away, she skirted around the passenger side of the truck to go on to her mother's car while Delilah squeezed the cart toward her side, giving a slight wave to the man as he waited for her to pass by before opening his car door. Hannah bravely lifted her gaze once again in his direction. He stepped out of the truck and closed the door. His sky-blue eyes grabbed hers, and he tossed her a slight smile before heading down the aisle toward the store's entrance. Hannah felt her face grow red by the returned attention, and she quickly fumbled for the car handle to slip inside the comfort of her mother's SUV.

Was she that hard up for attention since Greg left? Judging by his vehicle, he was probably in the blue-collar class. A factory job, no doubt, without even a college degree. Hardly the type for her by society's standards. After all, she was a law student, for the most part, despite the pause in her studies. She had every right to take a break. There was no shame in that. Her mother's entry into the car startled her, and she slipped on her seatbelt to regain her composure. "Ready?" Delilah smiled as she switched the vehicle's gear to reverse, enabling the backup camera.

Hannah nodded her head. "I'm eager to try out that color." Her eyes slipped over to the truck once more as they passed by it.

"Oh!" Delilah's voice perked up as she recalled a topic for discussion on the way back to the house. "For dinner tonight, I thought we try Mama's Place." She continued with a sly smile. "They have your favorite: baked spaghetti. Maybe even better than Vinni's back home."

Referencing the familiar Italian restaurant back on Long Island that her family frequented since she was a child. She was surprised it was still open, even as the owners aged. Their baked spaghetti was practically the only thing she ordered on the menu despite the various other options. She did sway a few times to split a pizza with her parents, but rarely.

"I don't know, Mom," Hannah teased with a grin. "You know I'm pretty inexorable when it comes to Vinni's."

"We can get it as takeout and watch another movie. I think we both will need a chance to relax once we finish with the bathroom." Delilah thumbed to the rear of the SUV, hinting at their project materials. "I've never really painted before."

Hannah shrugged playfully. "Neither have I. First time for everything."

January 9 Evening

Rejuvenated from the hot shower, Hannah walked back out of her room after getting dressed, to admire their handiwork for the day. The removal of the floral wallpaper was excruciating and more time-consuming than planned. They managed to take the first coat of paint before feeling way too passive to proceed further. Both were sweaty, hungry, and speckled with color. A dissolved lump of torn wallpaper was on the bathroom floor in their wake. Baked spaghetti grew on Hannah's mind as she remembered their dinner plans, and she was already salivating in anticipation. Her mom's door was still closed as she was getting dressed inside. The discarded pieces of wallpaper and paint containers remained on the paper-covered countertops and the protective paper flooring. She nodded her head in approval. Not too shabby for two inexperienced women at their first attempt that she recalled. A few little places to be touched up, but the second coat should fix most of it. She selected the color to be exceptionally well and a touching throwback to her grandmother's style. Minutes later, her mother hurried out of her room, scavenging through her purse to retrieve her dangling set of car keys and attached various assortment of key rings. "Ready?"

The idea of baked spaghetti for dinner was a boon to Hannah. The quick drive over to the restaurant was a bonus. A few cars were parked out front, and the brightly lit sign was warm and inviting. Grabbing her cross-body purse from underneath her passenger-side dash, Hannah slipped it over her as she proceeded to open her door hastily before giving her mother a chance to grab her purse. "I got it, Mom."

The move was unexpected, and it stumped Delilah, who sat there frozen in place. Her lower lip separated from the top in shock. "Are you sure?"

"Yeah," She tossed back a warm smile before closing the door and hugging herself as a shiver from the cold temperature worked its way down her body.

A bell chimed as she entered inside, and the place was bustling with waitresses and customers. Many were already seated in their comfy red booths while others staggered about, conversing in idle chatter while they waited for their seat or to pay their check. Fortunately, her mother called in the order on the way so that the wait wouldn't be as long. Sidestepping around a family of three waiting to be seated, she approached the counter, where a slim ivory-skinned midtwenties woman with curly mahogany hair greeted her with a smile. "How can I help you?"

"Pickup for Delilah," Hannah answered as she unzipped her purse to retrieve her wallet.

The woman turned around to the plastic bags line that contained orders with receipts stapled at the top. She retrieved one and set it on the counter in front of her, taking the receipt off the bag. The food's aroma aggrandized her hunger. She could see distinctively two foil-lined bowls with covers stacked on top of each other. "Seventeen eighty-three," the young lady said seconds later, after scanning the receipt into the register in front of her. Her face faltered with an awkward smile as Hannah obliged the unspoken request by handing her bank's credit card. "Uh, our card readers are down. I'm sorry. I forgot to say that up front. It's been a crazy night."

"You're serious?" the slightly aggravated tone echoed in Hannah's remark as she fumbled to slip her card back before moving to the compartment of her wallet that housed her paper money. Her fingers stopped when she noticed that she had six dollars in cash on her. Her mind raced as she felt the woman's green eyes staring at her for the payment. "I... uh, I don't have it. I'm going to have to go back out to the car," Hannah stumbled over her words as she felt embarrassed and ashamed. She wanted to do something good for her mother, and it turned out, her plans faltered because of lack of funds.

There was no empathy on the young girl's side as she shifted the bag to the right to set it aside. "All right. I do apologize. I'll hold your food here."

"Hey, Meg. Just stick it with mine," a man's voice behind Hannah intervened in the conversation.

Spinning on her heel, Hannah came face-to-face with a familiar stranger's smile and appearance. She saw the same man at the hardware store earlier that day, donning the same ball cap. She never got a stroke of real good luck at him until now. He was cute. In fact, very cute. His broad shoulders and athletic build displayed by a long-sleeved plaid shirt and dark denim jeans that perfectly fit his lower body. He was clean-shaven, with a few hints of stubble popping through the skin, and dirty blond hair that stuck out from his ball cap. A gorgeous smile flashed her way, and she realized that her heart was rapidly beating in her chest. "Thanks. I have half on me, and I'm sure I can get the rest out of the car."

He retrieved his wallet from his back pocket and thumbed through a few bills. "I got it."

Taking out her wallet once more, Hannah snatched her six dollars and held it out as he moved to her right side to pay the woman behind the counter. "At least let me give you what I have."

"Keep it." He waited for his change, then slipped it back into his wallet once more. "Visiting town?" He chuckled lightly. "I can tell by your accent. New York?"

"Yeah, Long Island. Visiting my mom here." Hannah left her response short and to the point. She didn't want to drag out her sob story to a total stranger, even if he was making a kind gesture. There was no doubt in her mind that she wanted to hit it off with him, but playing the pity card was not a way.

He chuckled again as he stuck the wallet back in his pocket. He picked up her bag and handed it to her. "Well, welcome to Wapak. Not much to look at."

Hannah found herself turning red by the statement as her mind slipped to something else. Conscious of her own words, she nodded her head and clutched the bag happily. "It's… uh, very different."

"Small town indeed. I saw you earlier at the hardware store," he purposefully pointed out. "I'm sure I'll run into you again."

"Yeah, I hope so." Hannah felt herself growing hotter at her own words, and her mind dashed to find a way to shore up her different meaning behind her true intentions. "I mean, probably will. We are doing renovations to Mom's old place." Feeling rather silly just standing there holding her bag of food, she chewed her lip and took a sideways glance at the restaurant's busy entrance. "Mom's waiting. I better head out. Thank you again."

He tossed a friendly wave as she felt his eyes and soft smile linger at her. "Good to meet you. The name's Jimmy."

"Hannah." Her back bumped into the door's handle as she turned back to look at him one final time. She scrambled to her mom's car and sat down rather quickly, still holding on to the bag of food. Her hands were shaking as her mind raced. All she could think of was Jimmy's warm smile at her.

She didn't realize that her demeanor was a little off in the car. "You okay, Hannah?" Delilah's voice reeled her back into reality.

"Yeah, I, uh, didn't have enough money. Their credit card machine was down." She avoided her mom's worried look as she set the food down safely between her heels as she slipped on her restraint.

Delilah was still stumped. "Do I need to go back in and pay for the rest of it?"

"No." Hannah shook her head. "A man offered to pay for it."

"A man?" Delilah cocked an eyebrow at the response.

On cue, Jimmy exited the restaurant and walked to where his truck was parked. Delilah caught Hannah's gaze, and a silly lopsided grin mischievously moved onto her face. "I get it," she teased. "He's kind of cute."

Hannah grew red in embarrassment. "Mom! Come on."

"Did you get his number?"

She playfully rolled her eyes. "I just broke up with Greg, remember? I'm not looking for anyone."

Delilah nodded her head in acknowledgment but wouldn't let up. "So? This guy was."

"I don't know Jimmy."

"You got his name."

Hannah laughed and swatted her mother's prying away. "Let's just go home. I'm hungry."

"Okay. Next time, get his number."

"There won't be even a next time."

"You never know."

January 11

The mini shopping trip to the mall in Lima seemed to allay Hannah's mind about her life's previous stressors. She was heading back in the car with her mother, with four bags containing various new outfit pieces. She splurged way too much as her thoughts tended to sway toward Jimmy. She privately hoped to catch his truck as they headed out that early morning, but to her disappointment, it was not in her sight. She began to debate about what Jimmy's type of girl would be defined as. Hannah was always into the latest fashions in New York. Her social media newsfeed filled with recommendations from models and other subject matter experts, pinning several that sparked her interest. Indeed, a man in a rural town didn't keep up with the trends. Or did he even care for all that? Was he more down to earth? Plain tastes? Simple? Could that even be her? That morning, as she was getting ready, she worked her long hair into a bun and slipped on a few silver dangling earrings. It had been weeks since she took the time to spruce up. A reflective smile gave her encouragement and hope as the morning's sun continued to rise. The temperatures were also spiking as a hot spell hit the area, making temperatures go well into the midfifties, and skies were clear—perfect weather for a car ride.

Delilah was humming to an old tune coming over the radio as their car slowed down to a stop at the red light. They were just entering the town of Wapakoneta, and familiar buildings were coming into view. Hannah was just starting to get her bearings. Still, with it being dark outside as the night came upon them, she felt like she was lost. Yawning, Hannah braced her head gently against the side window as she began to experience a feeling of lassitude. Both women were up at five that morning to head out for an all-day trip, even though Lima was not that far away. They planned to make the best of it. Just as she closed her eyes, a horrific screeching jerked her to alertness, followed by a violent crash. A large burgundy SUV T-boned a smaller gray sedan. The force caused the sedan to flip onto its right side, and metal cracked as the momentum still rocked the vehicle like a pendulum, back and forth, till the speed decreased. Smoke came out from under the SUV hood. The front end was pushed up against the windshield. Metal fragments of both vehicles littered the street at the point of impact. Traffic in both directions came to a grinding halt. The drivers jumped out of their cars to rush to assist. Sirens wailed in the distance. "Oh my god…" Delilah's words trailed off as she gaped at the horror. They were fortunate enough to be sitting off to the side to avoid any contact with the two vehicles, but another few minutes and that could have been her and her daughter.

Hot tears streamed down Hannah's face from the violence that she witnessed firsthand. Her body uncontrollably shook as memories of her dad's accident flashed into her vision, overcoming her true thoughts. Instead of strangers, all she could see was her dad's car in twisted metal. The remembrance of him broke her. She began to cry loudly as she hugged herself. Alarmed, Delilah turned to her. "Hannah! Hannah!" Her mother scrambled to comfort her, unbuckling her seatbelt. "Are you hurt?" Her eyes quickly surveyed for any sign of harm to her daughter on the passenger side.

Fervently shaking her head, Hannah choked up on her words as she continued to hold herself tightly, refusing her mother's solace. "I want to go home." Her words were struggling through the tidal waves of sobs.

Frowning at her daughter's behavior, Delilah hesitated to move away, still reaching out to her. "Hannah, honey. It will be okay…" She paused to allow her eyes to dart over to the accident scene to check on the status. It was hard to see the occupants of the vehicles by the crowd of onlookers and Good Samaritans. The crash was at a pretty high rate, so it may be in their best interest that there was a block from seeing the drivers' and passengers' fate.

Hannah refused to accept this answer. "I want to go home!" she demanded as she kept her eyes hidden in her hands. Her mind swirled like a whirlpool, and nausea hit her body.

Disturbed by all this, Delilah quietly refastened her restraint and maneuvered their car around the line of traffic to take an alternate route. An eerie calmness overcame the car's cabin. Two minutes later, she broke the silence between them, "We should be home in five minutes, honey."

Wiping her eyes as she finally was getting a handle on her sparked emotions, Hannah sniffed. "Not here."

"What?" Delilah allowed herself to take her eyes off the road to look over at her upset passenger. "What do you mean?"

"I want to go home, Mom," Hannah snapped, emphasizing the last word. "I want to go back to New York." Who was she kidding? Ohio was not even close to a good home for her. She refused to accept this. She wanted to return to New York. She longed for the way things were before. If only she could reset time a few months, she could find a way to save her dad. To keep the life that she once had.

Pulling into the driveway, Delilah sighed sadly as she turned off the ignition. "Sweetie, I know that the car accident was bad. I'm sure everyone survived." Trying to get a sense of where her daughter was coming from, intentionally not bringing up Robert's death. "It's been a long day. We all need the rest."

Ignoring her mom's recommendation, Hannah forcefully opened her car door, grabbing her things. "You can't force me to stay here." Her words were definitive. She didn't allow a response as she took out her own set of keys to unlock the house's door and retreat to the mock sanctuary of her bedroom. Not bothering to turn on the lights, she dropped her bags right when she walked in and slammed the door. A tiny night-light was the only beacon that created a way for her to see without colliding with anything. Tossing her body on the bed, she grabbed a pillow and pressed her face tightly against the soft fabric. There, she began to allow herself to weep once more. Deep down inside, she hoped that everything was a terrible dream. When she finally dared to reopen her eyes, she would find herself in her bedroom in Mastic, with her dad downstairs on the first level, brewing his morning coffee, when things were happier.

The darkness blocked all sense of time until she glanced at the brightly lit screen of her cellphone. She couldn't recall what time she arrived back at the house, but it felt like hours. Midnight was approaching. She thumbed through her contact list on her phone and came across her friend, Beth, who was still up in Manhattan. She was one of her classmates, and, just like Greg, she lost contact following her dad's passing. The two had a class together last semester and often hit up the café for lunch right before. Familiarity is what she desperately needed. Typing in a few words, she hit send and was relieved to see that the message was instantly read. A trail of dots showed that Beth was responding right away. To her surprise, the dots stopped and then a few seconds later, her phone's ringtone sparked to life. Alarmed by the sound, she fumbled to answer it. "Hello?" she softly asked in a whisper, hoping that the call wouldn't wake up her mother down the hall. She had no idea if she was still awake.

"Hannah! Where have you been? I've been so worried about you!" said Beth's thick New Jersey accent on the other side. "No text. No call. Not cool at all."

Hannah wanted to question why her friend didn't reach out to her if that was the case. However, she needed to confide in her, and starting things off with accusations was not the way. "Been hanging out with Mom here."

"Heard you and Greg broke up. Of course, I felt like an idiot when I ran into him after the break and asked how you were. He fucking bit my head off."

Hannah cringed at the news. Her heart sank deeper. "That bad, huh?" A beat. "Is he seeing someone else?"

"Have no clue. I don't see him anymore as I did. I doubt it." Her words left the possibility lingering in the air. "He sounded hurt. Did you break up with him?"

Even though the call was not video and Beth couldn't see her, Hannah shook her head in response. "It was… mutual. I just needed some time to work out things…" She frowned at the news. Was Greg's threat of going to his ex an empty threat? Or maybe he still wanted to be with her and wanted to give her time to get back to him once she came around? They left things pretty angrily. That was not an option on the table. She chewed her lip as she silently debated her next course of action.

"You coming back here, Hannah?" Beth's words were skeptical.

"I hope so… soon. Can I get with you tomorrow?"

"Um, sure. Talk to you soon."

Hannah quickly ended the call and scrolled through her contacts. Greg's number was still in there. She never bothered to delete it after their fallout. She pulled up a message and began to type away. Something casual like a check-in. She didn't want to give him the idea that she was crawling back to him. Yet she almost wanted to. Her thumb hesitated over the send button. What was holding her back? Retreating, she quickly discarded the message and locked her phone, tossing it to the side of the bed once more. Rolling onto her back, she sighed heavily as tiny droplets formed at her eyes once again. The darkness in the room wrapped all around her. She missed her life. She wanted to be resurrected. Why was she feeling like such a mess? Why such a kick of anxiety? She knew the car accident triggered a new sensation. But why? It was almost a month since her dad's death.

As a law student, she heard of conditions that many plaintiffs would bring up in personal injury cases, such as post-traumatic stress disorder. A common diagnosis following violent car accidents, otherwise abbreviated as PTSD. She never formally did get that diagnosis from her family doctor. She didn't think she needed the help of a physician or a psychologist. Grief was something that everyone had to deal with at some point in their lives, young or old. Society labeled the term as a mental illness with veterans who saw combat, IED impacts, or ambushes. She refused to accept this fact. This was something she refused to adapt to. She wanted her dad back. To feel his warm embrace wrap around her like when she was a little girl.

Right now, she was scared in the darkness. The solemn stillness of the house plagued her mind.

Her sorrow mutated into a strand of anger and frustration. She never considered herself to be a devout Catholic. She did attend mass from time to time with her parents when she was a child. After the separation, her dad simply lost the will to carry out the tradition. It had been years since she confessed her sins before the priest to seek remorse. Most disciplined Catholics would damn this act and shame her. She always heard the phrase "God has a plan for everyone." She couldn't come to grips with how this plan of his provided happiness and joy. Her question of the divine began to enrage her. Was this some punishment for her actions? For not confessing her sins? Not attending church services as she should? For not saving her virginity till after marriage? A harsh sentence to be carried out over a petty crime, she believed. As a student of law, she always wanted to believe in justice. How could this even be just? Or was her fate even more sadistic? Was this all on her own? If God was merciful, and this happened, did he indeed exist? Her family were not the model followers, but they were not blatant criminals. They did not commit crimes against another person. Why kill her father and leave her in despair? Was it to invoke fear? To make her fall to her knees and repent? Back to subjugation?

Clenching her fists tightly, feeling the nails dig against her skin, she rolled onto her right side as her eyes clutched tightly. She held back the newly formed tears. She was furious." Damn you…" she hissed menacingly through her gritted teeth. Her words were subjected to the deity. "I hate you! Why would you do this!" She sobbed over and over. If God truly existed, what did it mean for her father? Was he in the depths of hell for all eternity? Was he forever locked in chains? The grotesque image was plastered all over her mind. Grabbing her pillow, she hugged it tightly against her body and began to cry over and over. Finally, her body fell asleep—a welcoming refuge from the internal struggle.

February 4

Renovations around the house seemed ephemeral as the bathroom remained with only one paint coat, revealing various missed light spots—no other work done as time passed by. Reclusive, Hannah stayed tight to her cell, scrolling social media, reconnecting with all her classmates in New York, and staying up-to-date with Beth. When her mother came home in the evenings from work, she remained locked away in her room unless it was time to have supper, with little to no interaction. Her mother strived to strike up a conversation from time to time, but Hannah's responses were short, which often stirred the dialogue to a more hostile environment. Delilah was becoming irritable to the fact of her daughter's sudden mood change. At one point, she demanded to know the catalyst and discuss a way to work through it. Hannah refused. In her mind, there was nothing wrong with her. She was a daughter still mourning her father's loss and longing to be back home in New York. Her once belief of staying in Ohio seemed to be only a farce. The resilient mortar that founded the brick wall between them years ago seemed to be still intact despite the damage it took. Despite Delilah's explanation of the fallout, Hannah still blamed her. Delilah made a choice, and she would have to live with the everlasting effects. Hannah was the innocent victim of all the chaos.

Darkness and solitude were not the best ingredients for her. It gave her more time to think and only added in even more hatred and resentment. A tiny voice nagged her in the back of her mind, almost questioning her actions. They seemed to be shocked and almost appalled. Did she resent God and denounce him for her befalling? Her religious faith outlined that their heavenly father knew their lives' outcomes and choices before making them. If he saw this coming, why wouldn't he intervene? What kind of father would just sit there and let all the terrible chaos plague their child? Was her faith a complete lie? A manifestation solely by humankind for a sense of direction and purpose? Did God indeed exist? Is that the reason why all this was happening to her? With each passing day, she grew further and further from her mother and God. If her choices were her own, then she reserved the right to revoke her faith. As a Catholic, she never said her request to Jesus or God. It was always prescripted or led by the bishop during service. She could confess her sins if she would like to the father of the church. She knew other religious factions, such as Baptists and Methodists, did directly pray to God. Were they right to seek his wisdom? She was never a philosophical person to contemplate this. Would God even hear her plea if she outright questioned his motives or his existence? If she broke her Catholic rules and disobeyed, would it be another tick against her? The contemplation was over her head, and she felt like it was too much to put much energy into. She decided against all of it. She wanted to focus on other things, such as her plans with Becky and the semester to come. A much-needed announcement to be made to her mother. A light to the end of the darkness.

To her surprise, that Saturday afternoon, Delilah was knee-deep in the remodeling of her bathroom. She had on old jeans and a baggy long-sleeved button-up shirt. Her face was covered in sweat as she worked away at peeling away the layer of wallpaper. Hannah had no idea that her mother was continuing the project. She never mentioned anything to her about it. Then again, Hannah did shut her out for the second time. Standing still at the door frame, she let her eyes linger on her mother as the older woman worked away diligently. A messy pile of pieces of wallpaper strewn about beside her. "Hey, Mom…," she called softly to her.

Startled, Delilah quickly spun around, with part of the wallpaper still in her grasp. Strands of her hair came out from under the bun that she pinned earlier that day before work began. A look of worry crested over her sweaty brow. "Everything okay?"

Hannah couldn't tell if the expressed emotion was because of the surprise interaction or if her voice revealed a need for concern. "Yeah." Her almond-colored eyes glanced around at work done so far. "I didn't know you were going to start that next."

"I figured as much. Nothing else to do on this cold weekend." Her mother placed the discarded paper down in a pile next to her feet. Her words filled with sadness. "I didn't want to trouble you for assistance."

Hannah picked up on the pain and sighed heavily. "I'm sorry… I have just been going through a lot. I still miss him."

"I do too, honey. I know it's rough when you're so young."

"So you just accept it?" Hannah spat coldly. Her ill will toward God was churning inside her. She wanted to bust and express to her mother all the feelings and emotions that rocked her soul over the past few weeks—natural human emotions and yet challenging to contemplate on a superior level.

Shaking her head at the allegation, Delilah retired from her work. "Let's go out to the couch. Want some lemonade?" Hannah stepped aside to allow her mother to walk to the kitchen first while she remained in tow. After pouring two full glasses of lemonade, Delilah sat down at the circular wooden table in the kitchen's tiny dining area. Her eyes moved back her way as her fingertips interlaced around the cold glass in front of her. "I never will accept Robert's death. Just like I couldn't accept Mom's. I don't think the pain ever goes away. I know we each deal with it our way and that God has a plan for us all."

There it was—that reason. The same excuse planted and burned among many believers' minds. "Some plan," she scoffed. "Why would God even do this? Dad was no fucking criminal. Hell, he was good to us and you!"

She could see her mother cringe slightly at the sound of the swear words. Her mother never cared for it, but she was wise to choose her battles. There was a time and place for it. Inhaling sharply, then exhaling, she answered, "Sweetie, I know Robert was. I could never ask for more." There was a sliver of a twinkle in her eyes as she recalled a personal memory of their marriage. "Even after our marriage dissolved, there were no bad feelings towards one another. That was the kind of marriage that we had…" Tears formed in her eyes, and she sniffed quickly to delay them. "I sometimes want to believe he's still in New York. Working away at his desk and commuting in that awful traffic." A pause. "I don't miss that at all." She shook her head.

Hannah took a sip of the tangy beverage and then allowed her fingers to rest around the glass's rim. "Mom, I think I want to go back to New York for next semester… I'm ready." She dared not to lift her eyes as she spoke. She didn't want to see the pain in her mother's eyes—the resentment.

Nodding her head, Delilah lifted her chin to brave the news. "I know you are, sweetie. You have your own life…" She glanced around the kitchen as if she was trying her best not to break down then and there. "It's certainly not around here…" A short-lived feigned laugh escaped her lips at her joke. "There…" Delilah hesitated as she got up from her chair to retrieve a document from the counter before returning to the table once more. "There was an offer on the house. It came in yesterday, not even close to what I was hoping for. I don't think I'm going to take it." She looked across the wood surface at her daughter's displeased face. "Maybe I'll counter?"

The news was cringeworthy, and Hannah stared at her incredulously. "Are you toying with me?"

"What?"

"I know what you are doing…" Hannah hissed threateningly between clenched teeth. "You are trying to keep me stuck here… in this shithole."

"Hannah, you are not fair…I never said—"

She would not hear of it any longer! Shooting up from her chair, Hannah glared down at her. "You are not selling because you want me here to stay with you," she cut her off sharply. "What are you going to do? Throw some ridiculous offer at them to make the buyers go away? Then laugh?"

Her mother gaped at her. "Hannah, calm down. You're not even listening—"

"Oh, I am."

"No, you're not!" Delilah's elevated voice made the whole area grow silent in the house. A distant tick of a grandfather's clock was the only noise heard coming from the living room. Her chest was heaving as the stress mounted. "I want to sell the house to help you. I know all of the estate money would be going into a trust fund that you can only draw out so much at a time and that your tuition is paid for. You won't have the means to survive up there by just that for now…" Standing up from the table, she leaned over and embraced her daughter tightly as tears finally were allowed to pour down her face. "You are young, sweetie. I want you to live your life. Enjoy your youth…"

The overbearing wave of emotions was infectious, and Hannah felt her hot tears moving down her face as well. "Mom, I'm so sorry… I'm so sorry…"

"Shh, don't be. It's okay."

Shaking her head, Hannah continued to sob, "No, I am. I shouldn't act this way to you; none of this is your fault. Why? Why did this happen to him? To us?" Her mind flashed to her earlier religious-themed internal debate. "Why did God allow this? Is he even real!" She could hear her voice screaming at the top of her lungs on the last two questions as she choked. She clutched onto her mother's shirt desperately like an infant who had just fallen and received an injury. She needed that. She needed the comfort of a mother to a child right now—her mother.

"It will be okay… Shh…" Delilah cooed gently. Her voice the only sound heard now in the house. Hannah disembarked from the hug as she took a step back to wipe away their tears with a faint smile. "Your father would be so proud of what all you have accomplished, Han. Don't ever give up. You are strong. You are powerful. Understand?" She clasped her daughter's hands with her own, squeezing them gently. Biting her lip to suppress any more tears,

Hannah returned the squeeze and nodded her up and down as her hands lingered in her mother's.

Later on, that afternoon, Hannah and Delilah were heading back to the hardware store to pick up another gallon of paint. Hannah slowed the vehicle down as she approached the red light at the intersection. There was a calmness to her, like the gentle breeze along a beach after a hurricane passed. Her heart still ached as it recovered from the devastation, and her soul seemed unsteady from her inner struggle that manifested. Suddenly, the sound of a car horn beeping nearby startled her. Her mind raced back from her thoughts as she spotted a familiar pickup crossing in front of her. It was Jimmy. He too noticed her and was looking right at her as he waved. Her heart lurched in her chest, and she returned the wave sloppily as the timing caught her off guard. Her eyes remained on his vehicle as it continued down the road, as the sight of him enthralled her. Delilah grinned at the flirtatious exchange. "Him again?"

Feeling herself become red and realizing that her light changed over to green, Hannah let off the brake and back on the accelerator as she continued their trek. "Come on, Mom." She tossed the figurative meaning away playfully. "I'm sure he's nice."

"And cute?" her mom chided.

Shaking her head, Hannah laughed at the apparent fact. "I don't know him. Besides, I seriously doubt he's a college grad or even going to college. And certainly not the only boy in town." As she spoke, she wasn't too sure if her argument's merits were more in line with her mother's or with herself. Was she downplaying all this to remain hopeful for Greg? He never texted her since their breakup, but then again, Beth did state that she didn't see him with anyone else. Maybe Greg had a change of heart? Perhaps he did want her back and was waiting for her to make the next move? She glanced down at her cell securely stashed away in the center console. A nagging urge to text Beth for any updates surfaced. Once they reached the hardware store, a quick text wouldn't hurt.

"Why does that matter?" Delilah took up devil's advocate, continuing their debate.

"Because… I mean, I would want someone who has a college degree like I'm shooting for." The counter threw Hannah off course, and she almost missed her turn into the store's parking lot. A more brutal bump jolted the vehicle and made her grit her teeth. "Ugh, sorry."

Remaining quiet, Delilah nodded her head in acknowledgment. She remained poised until the vehicle parked, and she unfastened her seatbelt. "In some things, degrees aren't everything. After all, he's not applying for a job with you." She flashed a warm smile at her daughter. "Think about it."

"Mom." Hannah rolled her eyes playfully. "I'm not even looking right now." She lied as she reached to grab her cell, not giving up on her earlier undisclosed plans.

"Who says you have to be?"

February 10

Her smile, in the mirror, appeared luminous. Picking up her hairbrush, she began to gently stroke through her long locks as she admired a new soft burgundy long-sleeved tunic. It fit just perfectly over her midthighs as her black leggings were seen after that. The pants raced down into her, gray-toned winter dressed-down faux fur boots: a favorite outfit that she bought from the shopping spree with her mother in Lima. She was surprised that her mother mentioned her accompanying her to her worship service at the local church that morning. The biggest surprise of it all was that her mother was going to a Baptist church and not Catholic. Her mother never talked about her personal religious beliefs before Robert came along.

Hannah assumed there was no transformation over to Catholicism. But in fact, her mother converted soon after she and Robert were engaged. She grew up Baptist, and her childhood church was much smaller than the one she currently attended. Robert was a devout Catholic at the beginning of his law career, and the church's requirement to bless the marriage was that the bride had to convert and raise the children in the same faith. There was no hesitation in Delilah's decision since she loved Robert, and she could still believe in God. He didn't mind her still saying her nightly prayers. Conversion to the Catholic faith was a big deal for him and his family. It took Hannah a few months to adapt to the change, and she constantly had to get Robert's help memorizing all the prayers.

The idea of going to another church was appealing to Hannah. She always seemed curious about exploring other cultures and beliefs. The best part of growing up in New York was that it was a melting pot for all races, cultures, religions, and sexual orientations. Acceptance was second nature for the majority of the populace. The church they would be attending that morning was called Celestial Baptist Church, named for the town's pride in knowing that a famed astronaut named Neil Armstrong grew up there. A small museum was one of its biggest attractions there. The newly developed church was located just two miles out from the main thoroughfare before the never-ending rows of fields used for growing corn and soybeans. They just had celebrated their second anniversary with a large fall festival for the entire congregation in September. Hannah couldn't believe how large the building was! The parking lot was almost as big, with rows and rows filled with cars for the earlier services. Her heart leaped for excitement, like a small child taken to an amusement park for the first time. Her mother nervously unhooked her belt once parked and glanced at her daughter's way. "You sure you're okay about coming here?" Hesitation rested on her tongue's tip.

"Why wouldn't I be? Looks fun." Her daughter nodded her head in admiration.

"Well, it's much different than what you're used to. We have live music."

"Like a choir?" Hannah bundled herself up to brace for the chilly weather outside the vehicle.

"No," her mother chuckled as she followed suit. "They have a band, like guitars and drums. You will like it."

"That should be interesting." Hannah giggled as she let her mom take the lead to go inside. Many goers were exiting their vehicles to make their beeline to several of the church's entrances. Delilah was going to the main one and politely waved to two women handling the door, handing out programs, and greeting every attendee.

Inside, Hannah navigated the crowds of people who were exiting or stopping to chat with friends; she hoped she wouldn't lose Delilah in the waves of people! The church interior opened up to more doors that revealed a large room that housed rows of cushioned seats and a balcony that housed more. Her eyes became wide in the vastness of it. It felt like she was going to some big movie complex or a concert! She never was inside a church so big! Finding an empty row near the center about three aisles down, Delilah sat down in the seat near the walking path while Hannah took her left side. Few waved to Delilah and greeted her return as they went to find their places. Delilah opened her program to scan over the agenda before picking up her purse to rummage for her wallet. Hannah looked on with interest. "This is so big!" she exclaimed.

Her mother nodded in agreement as she took out a twenty-dollar bill and placed it inside the envelope tucked in the pamphlet. She could tell her daughter was watching her. "It's the offering," she whispered.

"Oh… um." Hannah unzipped her purse and retrieved her own twenty dollars. "Here."

Delilah held up her hand to refuse her gesture. "I got it, sweetie."

"Come on…," Hannah urged lightly as she waved the bill more in her mother's face.

Defeatedly, Delilah placed her bill inside and then sealed it. "That was nice of you…" She smiled warmly at her.

Minutes later, the lights grew dim, and the band began to play onstage. There were two guitarists, one drummer, one working a keyboard, while a man and woman stood at the center, with wireless microphones. The woman's voice dominated over the music as she spoke, "Let's worship today."

"Stand." Delilah tapped her daughter to follow the crowd in unison. Hannah fumbled to set her stuff on the floor beside her before standing to join in. She remained quiet as the worshippers began to sing along with the song playing. Giant display screens displayed the lyrics, but Hannah never heard the hymns before. She stood there in silence and just listened along. A grin appeared on her face as her mom sang along with passion and joy. Despite the singers over the speakers, the only voice she could hear was her mom's angelic tone. It was so harmonic and resonated inside her.

After several worship songs, announcements, and offerings, the service proceeded as a man in his early fifties strolled onto the stage, with a black leather-bound Bible tucked away under his arm. He was dressed in casual jeans, boots, and a navy blue polo shirt. He greeted the congregation with a friendly, quick wave before opening the Bible on the pulpit. The atmospheric tone was down to earth and laid back. Not even as formal as a class lecture. That wasn't the thing that compelled Hannah the most to do what she did following the sermon. It was the topic. The pastor called out a particular verse from the book of Isiah 41:10. He read the passage word for word until he broke it apart out of its context. The message was about fear, angst, and dismay. The purpose was so captivating that her attention grasped at it, yearning to know more.

As if the Holy Spirit was speaking to her directly instead of indirectly. It moved her. Then guilt washed over. The ocean of void pulled her in deeper and deeper like a strong rip current. She managed to swim out of it before, but not unharmed. She remembered. She remembered the words. Her words. Her questioning of God's plan for her. His sole existence. Every human goes through trials and tribulations, just like Jesus did before his death and resurrection. A test of their faith. She cringed at her failure. She denounced him. She almost wanted to damn him. Damn him for taking her father away too soon, shaking her entire world into a mess. As she in her chair, mulling over her past transgressions, she began to shrink. She had no right to be there. If only Delilah knew what thoughts hit her mind. She would never offer to take her daughter to join in the praise. What right did she have?

Her conscious stole the time, and she was alarmed when suddenly the band struck up in the background as the pastor's message was coming to a close. Their tune quiet but indicating what was to come. The pastor's warm smile spanned from left to right. He reiterated God's love and wisdom over the uncertainty of fear and anxiety. He called to his congregation not to revel in what the Devil wanted but to trust the heavenly Father. As the music began to pick up, he reminded the church of his invitation: to come to him with their sorrows and troubles. He would pray over them, help them find their way. There would be no shaming over their sin. All would accept them for they were all sinners. The band took over, and everyone stood up once more to sing the final hymn. Hannah shot up this time before her mother. A spark of affinity toward the church churned.

A calling to her soul. Her feet moved before she said to her mom over the loud singing, "I'm going up there." Delilah squeezed back against her chair to allow passage. Breathing faster, Hannah continued her path down the aisle, keeping her eyes centered on the pastor standing there with open arms. She grew shy as she felt the congregation's eyes glancing in her direction. The man took her hand and gave it a soft encouraging squeeze. A few others made a beeline to the front as well. All knelt on the plush green steps that led up to the stage, with their heads bowed. A few moved from their pews to place their hands on their repenting backs in a show of compassion as they silently prayed along with them. This moved Hannah. The pastor eyed her confusion and smiled warmly at her. "Let's go out and chat." He motioned for another gentleman to take his place as the worship song was winding down to a close.

The hallway outside the main area was brightly lit and rowed with different offices. A few backstage hands were standing at the ready. They greeted Hannah with jubilation and a friendly wave. "I'm Pastor Samuel Hicks of Celestial. You must be new." The pastor turned back to address her before opening his door to his office. "Please come inside. I have tea and coffee if you would like to have some, and a few of the donuts made their way back here." He chuckled in delight, "I think they wish to fatten me up."

The small talk calmed her nerves, and Hannah sat down in a chair. The office contained a small computer desk that took very little space, while the majority of the room held a bookshelf with rows and rows of biblical works, two chairs like the one she was sitting in, and even a couch. Framed works of art with inspiring messages lined the walls. "So... Miss?" Samuel vamped up the conversation once more as he sat down in the chair, approximately four feet from her.

"Hannah... Hannah Marks. I'm visiting today with my mother, Delilah Marks."

"Delilah?" He nodded his head by the name. "I'm so glad that she's back with us... It's been a while. I am sorry for the tragedy that struck your family. I lost my father five years ago. Every day is a struggle."

"It is…," she agreed as she rubbed her arms nervously.

"So, Ms. Marks, I'm sure Jesus is overwhelmed by pure joy to know that you found the courage and strength to join us here at Celestial. We all hope your journey with us will continue. We would love to have you here with your mother. Did you need to speak with me about anything that is weighing down on your heart?"

Pausing, Hannah took a breath and stared at him so hard that it felt like she was going to look right past him. Everything bubbled to the surface. She felt so silly just venting to a total stranger, even if he was a man of the cloth. Then again, she did yearn to confess her sins even though she was not Baptist. She wasn't too sure how to do this. Stumbling over her thoughts, she babbled, "I don't know how… see, I'm Catholic and I—"

"I see," he acknowledged, with a head nod. "I agree. Baptists can be very different. Yet I believe our missions are the same. I'm here to listen to anything that is burdening your soul."

Hannah cringed at the term. She lowered her eyes. How could she atone for what she said earlier? There was hope in Pastor Hicks's words. Would his acceptance indeed be there? How could anyone of his stature simply accept that a fellow believer firmly denounced the existence of their creator? Their Father? Trembling, she placed her hands on her knees as her voice quivered, "I think I'm going to hell…" A beat. There was silence on his end, but she could tell he was attentive to her matters of utmost importance. She continued, "I'll tell you everything… I need to tell someone."

"Go ahead."

March 10

"Guess what." Delilah's playful tone grabbed Hannah's attention from the stove that evening. She turned slightly to see her mother waiving the back of an envelope, purposely hiding the label. "You have mail."

"The school!" Hannah accepted the mail article as she stepped aside to allow her mother to take her place to hover around their supper that was still cooking away. Tearing into the envelope delicately to not rip the contents, Hannah could feel her heartbeat accelerating. A few weeks previously, she reached out to the school to see if she could enroll in fall classes. The registrar confirmed everything with her over the phone and stated they would send out a letter to verify her acceptance once they check everything. She knew she was a shoo-in to get back in with the college, but there was always the possibility that something could go awry. Her luck was not the best in the past few months. Her hands trembled; her eyes raced across the body of the letter. She was in! The zenith of her year so far! Squealing out in triumph, she embraced her mother, with tears flowing down her face. Not in anguish as she was accustomed to, it seemed, during her endurance of the calamity that befallen her; instead, they were of pure joy.

Delilah returned the hug tightly and said softly to her, "Hannah, I am so proud of you. Your father would be too. He always wanted you to follow him in his footsteps. You are getting there."

Breaking away, Hannah wiped out the remnants from her eyelids and clutched the letter to her heart. "Thank you, Mom." Her eyes lifted in the woman's direction, apologetic. "You have been so good to me. I don't deserve this, not by the way I acted towards you."

"Hush." Her mother shook her head. "You are smart, Hannah. You do deserve this. You work hard. You always have." A wide smile moved across her face. "We need to go celebrate." She moved over to remove their food from the stove. "My treat."

Laughing at the change, Hannah nodded her head in glee. "Yeah, let me text Beth real fast. She's going to be ecstatic!"

As soon as they got back home that night, she crashed onto the bed, with a stomach filled with delicious steak and a few drinks. The euphoria from the mixture of excitement and alcohol placed her on cloud nine. She promised Beth that she would call her that evening as soon as she got back. She couldn't wait until the next day to discuss their plans. She seemed more at peace with her decision despite the small glimmer of sadness from knowing she would be apart from her mother during her semester. With their house now sold, her mother would continue to reside in Ohio. Hannah accepted this decision without resentment. She had changed since their first latest interaction. Since discovering the new church with her mother a few weeks ago, they consistently attended the following few Sundays. Her Catholic upbringing complicated it, but the positive and welcoming atmosphere made the adaptation easier. Her soul was in harmony, and she felt God's blessing down on her. No more disarray. Beth picked up the call on the second ring, her voice high-pitched in matched excitement. "You are coming back!"

Staring up at the ceiling, keeping the cell at her right ear, Hannah sighed in happiness. "Yeah. I'm ready, and we can hang out so much!"

"Wait till you see my place. We will need to decorate. I always wanted you as a roomie. I already put you on the sign-up sheet, so you are good to go. So you going to come to visit during the break to check it out?"

"That shouldn't be a problem with Mom…" Hannah's words trailed off as she bit her lip. Ironically, she was in the same predicament as Greg, the catalyst for their breakup. The return to New York was rough. Just the thought of it made a knot form in her stomach. What was she so afraid of? At first, she dared not to leave the city that never slept; now that she was away, she feared returning. The strand of excitement appeared to be evanescent. Greg's name echoed in her mind. "You have seen him?" The words spewed out of her mouth before she was able to stop, subconsciously thinking him back into existence.

"Who?"

"Greg. I mean, is he still around?" Hannah remained hopeful.

She could almost see the sly smirk on her friend's face over on the receiving end. "I have." Her voice was playful and teasing. "Not with anyone. Should I tell him the good news?"

Hannah felt herself grow red and hot in the face. Why did she feel this way? He was the one who pressured her and didn't understand, or he didn't try to understand. Then again, she bathed in guilt as she contemplated on it some more. Maybe it was all her fault? Maybe she was acting selfishly? Perhaps this was a second chance. He wanted her back in the bustling metropolitan area. He was getting his wish after all. The thought of being in his arms again made her yearn for him. It had been nearly five months since their last intimate session. Not like she craved sex all the time like some of her friends in Manhattan. Beth was one of those girls. As soon as she dumped one boyfriend, she was on to the next within days. Her carefree lifestyle was an acquired taste. One that did not set suitable for Hannah. She blamed this thinking upon her religious upbringing; then again, she didn't save herself for marriage, which was a huge sin in the eyes of most of the faith. Her silence only added spice to Beth's tone. "I take that as a yes."

"No!" Hannah busted out finally, regaining her composure. "Not yet. Let me make sure that…"

Beth seemed to revel in her problem with a peal of laughter. The torment was brutal. "Relax. I'm just playing. If I see him, I'll just tell him that I talked with you and that you are coming back in the fall. I won't drop anything else."

She sighed in relief as the tension rolled off her shoulders. "Thank you."

"Text me when you make the flight. I'm so excited! Talk to you later."

"Yeah, you got it." Hannah forced herself to share the same enthusiasm as her friend, but deep down, regret was settling in. The same uneasy feeling she had when Greg was prodding her about coming back to visit. If she was trying to get on his good side, finding out that she would happily agree to fly in to see her best friend but not him was not the way to approach this. Then again, he could be involved, and Beth did not know about it, or maybe Beth was kind in trying not to hurt her. What about Jimmy? Her timid subconscious spoke to her. It seemed like he had some type of interest, but it was just casual flirtatious waves. She hadn't run into him for weeks, despite the town being much smaller than where she was from. Maybe Jimmy was only confused. Maybe it was her loneliness trying to replace whatever she lost with Greg. She knew nothing about Jimmy, and the fact that she didn't see him clearly could mean he was heavily involved with someone else. Taken or not, sometimes, men love to flirt. He could be hiding it. Passing Greg up another time would not be wise if allowed to reconcile their relationship. Yawning, she felt exhaustion creep in as she realized just how late it was getting. Setting her phone down, she closed her eyes and let her mind continue to process it all while she slept. Delilah would not be opposed to the idea of her flying out to see Beth in the upcoming weeks. She had to make her flight arrangements soon. Everything was piecing together. Mending the break and healing now, it seemed without complication. Smiling warmly in the darkened room, Hannah snuggled against her pillow as she got more comfortable, "Goodnight, Dad. Thank you. I love you."

March 15

Despite the flux in temperatures that were abnormal for the season, there was still a chill in the morning air as Hannah moved the car's window down a few inches to feel the breeze. Her quotidian routine included dropping her mother off at her office before tending to a few errands or having some personal time. That morning would be somewhat different. The night before, she purchased her round-trip ticket to fly from Dayton to La Guardia in two weeks. Sheer excitement made her temperament jolly, a complete one-eighty over the past few months. After they stopped in the parking lot, Delilah paused to exit out of the passenger side and turned back around to face her daughter. "Have fun shopping." Hinting at Hannah's plan that day to travel to Lima once more to find outfits to take with her on her trip. Her time away would only be four days. Her itinerary consisted of meeting up with Beth once she landed, checking out her apartment, catching up, and meeting up with the college's registrar to discuss her course credits. Digging into her purse, Delilah flashed a fifty-dollar bill her way. "Here."

"Mom." Hannah swatted her hand away playfully. "I have my own money." Despite not being employed, she did have at least two thousand left in her savings account after purchasing the plane ticket.

Delilah shook her head by her resistance and stuffed the bill in her hand. "Take it. I know that you never have any parsimony. You may need extra spending money for accessories."

Reluctant, Hannah accepted the gift and placed it in the car's front console for the time being. "Thanks, Mom." Waving, Delilah got out and pulled her purse's strap over her shoulder. "Love you!"

There was a twinkle in her mother's eye from her daughter's affirmation. "Love you, sweetie. Be safe."

Exiting the parking lot, she switched the radio station that played more of the current pop hits and used the onboard vehicle's navigation system to direct her toward the interstate. Three minutes out from her turn to the on-ramp, a car to her right caught her eye. She glanced over to see Jimmy turning across the street into the parking lot of the hardware store. Her heart lurched at the sight, and she felt herself grabbing the steering wheel tighter. Frantic, Hannah checked her mirrors and took a quick lane change to turn left at the intersection to follow him in. He was already parking near the upper side of the parking lot, with several empty spaces nearby, and she searched for one that wouldn't be too obvious. Skirting up inside an area that was five spaces up from his truck, she quickly checked her appearance in the mirror and glanced in his direction. He was getting out of his vehicle and stuffing his wallet in his back pants pocket, not even looking in her direction. Her pulse raced. He didn't see her! Biting her lip, she toyed with the notion of walking right up to him. She had to clear the air. Was she stalking him? Knowing she would miss perhaps her only chance, she gathered up her purse and phone and quickened her steps to follow him. Glancing at her phone, she pretended to not be paying attention should he look back to see her following him in. *What are you doing, Hannah? This is nuts. You are acting so childish!* Ignoring her inner voice, she noticed the date on her phone. March 15. *Beware of Ides of March.* She scoffed at the old history lesson from high school—the prophet's iconic phrase given to Julius before his untimely death. A foreshadow to the ill that would befall him. A chill went up to her cervical spine. She shook it off, a coincidence and nothing more. She would not be spooked! "Hey, Jimmy!" Finding her voice just when she was about fifteen feet behind him.

In front of her, the athletic ball-capped man stopped and turned back with first a look of confusion, then a smile when he saw her walking his way. She purposefully slowed her pace as she tucked her phone away in her purse. "Hey, you."

"Funny to see you here," Hannah stumbled with her words to strike up the conversation.

"Yeah, I have to pick up a few things for the house. You?" He motioned with his head for her to walk beside him as he continued to the store's entrance.

"Mom and I are renovating her house. I need to pick up a gallon of paint," she lied, using their previous purpose there—a buyable reason.

"You painting?" he chuckled playfully, then stopped in midstride. "Hold up."

She stopped suddenly. "What is it?"

Jimmy cleared his throat, then switched positions with her to place her on the inside of the travel aisle. He took the outside. "Sorry. Raised to always keep the woman out of harm's way." He chuckled. "Though with the cars backing up without looking, I don't know what side is best at odds."

Moved by this, Hannah smiled warmly at him. A kind and unexpected gesture. She glanced over at the rows of cars pulled into their spaces as the pair strolled by. "I think you may be safer over there, Jimmy." Smirking, tossing his name out in a flirtatious manner. "You know I still owe you for dinner the other night." Letting the unspoken request linger in the air.

He paused to allow her to enter the store before proceeding behind her. "Nah, I told you that it was on me."

Desperate, she blurted out, "What if I cooked you something?" She inwardly cringed, knowing she didn't have any culinary skills.

Jimmy bit the bait. "What are you having?"

Tossing her head side to side to think of something in a casual manner, she tried to narrow down a few of his preferences by what little she knew of him. "Steak?" Tossing out the prominent manly item.

He grinned at her. "Never had a girl cook steak for me. Sure." She turned red at his grin. *God, he is gorgeous.* She almost felt like she was transforming into a puddle. Giddy like a young teenager in high school, swooning over the captain of the football team. His charming facial features were so captivating that she felt herself becoming lost in his eyes. "I'd never turn down a free meal. What day would work for you? I would be glad to hang out rather than at the hardware store."

Realizing that she was standing there, staring blankly at him, Hannah recomposed herself and fumbled at the reality of time. "This Saturday evening?" A three-day notice to her mother of her stupid desperation was plenty of time to make this work.

"Sounds perfect. Let me take down your cell so we can stay in touch, and I'll get the address later." He slipped his cell out of his front pants pocket and began to type away with his fingers.

"Sure, and I'm staying with Mom. She lives like three blocks from the high school."

He nodded his head. "I know the area. I work ten minutes away from there."

"Oh?" She perked up with the opportunity to learn more about him.

"Yeah, Carter's Industrial. I make wiring harnesses. It sucks, but it's good pay around here. The hours suck. Have to be in by four in the morning."

She scrunched her nose at this. Not the occupation, but the time of day. "I can't even function then."

He laughed at her comment. "I don't think I can."

The pause in their conversation became awkward. Hannah wanted to hang out with him more, but following him around the store did seem pretty strange. "Well, um, I better get the paint for Mom."

"Yeah, I almost forgot what I came in here for," he chuckled, with a smile, rubbing the back of his neck as his eyes glanced around the store's open space. "I'll text you later?"

"You better," she teased as she tossed a wave before heading in the direction of the paint section. Thank goodness she knew her way there so he wouldn't find out her fabricated lie. Once she was satisfied to see him out of her vision, she quickly made a beeline for the store's exit and back to her car. She giggled as she sighed happily.

The pause in her trip did delay her to Lima, but it was so worth it. Settling back down in her driver's seat once she made it to her mother's SUV, she sighed again as she looked down the aisle toward the store once more. Her mind thought back to the quick exchange. "It was so worth it." The somewhat date was another driving factor in making her buy some new wardrobe. She couldn't wait to tell her mom the unexpected good news when she got off work that evening.

March 18

The run-in with Jimmy at the hardware store was very fortunate for Hannah. She finally got the opportunity to get an impending question out in the open, and the answer was in her favor! Now it seemed like time was abating as she hurried around the kitchen that evening to grill the steaks on the stove. Delilah was at her house while the two conquered the daunting task together. Neither was a grill master. Robert was always the one operating the outdoor grill during their cookouts. Even when it rained, he took to the stove to deliver the best-tasting steaks that one could ever savor. There was no other. Jimmy was to arrive in fifteen minutes, and she felt like she had five minutes left. Sweat dripped down her body from the heat of the stove, and she could feel her makeup liquifying on her face. Her heart raced as each minute ticked away. That was the current status since nine that morning. She was so nervous! As if she was attending her senior prom all over again. "Hannah, you're burning the steaks." Delilah's comment jerked her out of her thoughts, and she quickly pulled the frying pan away as smoke came from underneath the meat.

"Damnit!" she cursed as she took her spatula to check the underside of the steak for damages. Thankfully, it was a little blackened, but only one piece suffered. She would take that one, already deciding that the best-looking one among the three would be stowed for Jimmy. She needed to impress since this shindig was her idea. What did she get herself into?

Gently holding her hand over her daughter to take over, Delilah chuckled at her daughter's frenzy. "Go freshen up before he gets here. I'll finish it."

"Thanks, Mom!" Hannah kissed her mother on the cheek, then hurried down the hallway to her bathroom to fix her makeup and apply another coat of deodorant, with a few dashes of her body spray. Body odor was not a turn-on. She stared into the mirror at her pure complexion to check out what she needed to correct before grabbing her caboodle. "Okay, okay," she sighed gently to compose herself. "Get it together, Hannah. Just a cute boy. You got this." Her hands shook as she took out her makeup brushes to dash on a few splotches of her foundation to cover the imperfect areas, then switched over to another layer of her cherry blossom lip gloss. Smacking her lips slowly together, she admired her newly fixed-up appearance and smiled big. "Hey, Jimmy," she flirtatiously spoke to her reflection. "It's nice to see you." Shaking her head vigorously in disapproval, she groaned and then slammed her hands on the bathroom counter to regain her strength. Taking a deep breath, she finally lifted her head to glance at her image once more. "Hey. Glad you could make it." Pausing her head, she rocked her head from side to side to consider her tone. "Not bad. Not too desperate and not too cold. Hard to get." She gave herself a playful wink. Glancing down at her cell, she checked the read time of their last text together. He reached out to her to say that he was leaving his house and would be over shortly. He was running a bit late because he got held over at work and needed to get home to clean up. She could almost imagine him racing to the shower and stripping his clothes off to hop in. She bit her lip as she could almost see his naked frame in pure view. From what she saw so far, he did have a captivating body. The idea of him in the nude made her blush despite not being a virgin anymore. Not like she had never been with a man or had never seen one naked. Still, the concept of Jimmy naked and wet in the shower was enticing and made her giddy. Smiling inwardly, she wondered if he felt the same about her. Did he think the same perverted thoughts? The chime from the doorbell grasped her attention, and she raced out of the bathroom, slamming her hand against the switch to cut off the lights. "I got it!"

Stopping right outside the door, she did a final check before opening it. Jimmy was on the other side, in a pair of dark denim jeans, a black-and-gray long-sleeved flannel button-up shirt with a black shirt underneath. The ball cap was off his head, finally revealing the thick dirty-blond hair underneath. In his hand was a small bouquet of roses: three white ones and three light-pink ones. With a handsome smile, he handed the item to her. "Hey. Thanks for having me up."

A warm sensation moved down her body by his presence, and she was touched already. Accepting the gift, she politely admired the roses before stepping aside to let him in. "Thanks. You didn't have to."

"I'm getting a free meal. I need to provide something." He gave a playful wink as he walked inside before she closed the door to block the chilly evening air.

Delilah peeped out from the kitchen to greet the guest with a wave. The delightful smell of the prepared steak and side dishes was powerful and making Hannah grow hungrier. "Hello. I'm Delilah. Hannah's mother. You are very welcome to join us. It will be ready in just a minute."

Growing red in embarrassment, Hannah piped up, "Mom is helping me grab the plates," hoping that her mother would shun her, crediting the preparation of their meal. Ushering him to the table, she dashed off to the kitchen to catch a breath and grab some drinks. Her heart was racing out of her chest. Pausing at the kitchen's entrance, she glanced in her mother's direction, and her mother, in turn, gave her an encouraging thumbs-up. Realizing that she forgot to take his drink order, she moved out again to where he was sitting. "Uh, sorry. What did you want to drink?"

"Pop or beer," he chuckled. "I'm not picky."

She was teetering her head some, hearing the terminology reference to soda, and she moved back to retrieve a requested item from the fridge. Taking another deep breath, she slowed herself down before bracing back into the dining area. "Here goes."

The meal took less than fifteen minutes to finish, and Hannah felt like she inhaled her food. She mentally kept reminding herself to slow down. Now and then, in between bites, she would catch his charming eyes or smile. "Can I get you anything else to eat or drink, Jimmy?" Delilah finally broke the silence in the room.

He held up his hand to gently refuse the offer. "I overate than I should already," he chuckled. "You sure know how to cook steak, Hannah." Adding playfully, "I think I should come over here more often for my meals."

"Glad you enjoyed it." Hannah giggled, hiding the secret that her mom did most of the cooking.

So, Jimmy," Delilah began, "tell me more about yourself. Are you a student, or do you work somewhere?" The casual talk was over, and now it was time for the grilling, with Delilah being the overprotective parent of their child. Most of the time, when it came to daughters, it was the father's prerogative to interrogate the prospective suitor to see if they were well matched for their child. Robert was always that way. The ironic thing is that he never really knew much about Greg while he was alive. He knew that Hannah was seeing him, but she never brought him around to have the meeting's formal session. Delilah stayed out of it and only gave her words of wisdom. After all, Hannah was of age, and their restrictions could only go so far. Still, as a parent, she wanted to learn more about the man that took an interest in her daughter. She had to step into Robert's shoes.

"Never went to college. I took on a job right out of high school, at the factory. Temporary turned into long-term." Jimmy redirected the question in Hannah's direction. "You have to be a graduate. What's your degree?" His eyes were twinkling right at her.

Hannah sat up straighter to address the question, pausing to glance in her mother's direction. She wasn't quite sure how to answer. His response was distracting her thoughts. She figured he had no former higher education other than high school, a conscious discriminative notion by the town's comparison to Manhattan. She had him pegged. That wasn't what suddenly bothered her. What would her mother think? A noncollege-educated man? Realizing that everyone was waiting on her answer, she stuttered as her words clambered back to her thought, "I'm still in law school… technically. I took the current semester off…" Pain washed over. "My dad was killed in a car accident near Christmas..." She held herself firmly together as she gathered her inner strength to get through the complicated feelings deep inside. "I took the semester off to spend time with Mom."

"She got accepted to their fall semester," Delilah finished the response off with a positive note. Though Hannah wasn't sure if its meaning was positive or a way to advise Jimmy that her time there was only temporary. She cringed at the double meaning and almost loathed how her mother brought that firm reminder out in the open. She held her breath.

To her shock, the man did not sway away. He acknowledged the statement with a nod of his head. The same smile never disappeared from his clean-shaven face as he glanced at her once more. "A lawyer? Very impressive. I better watch myself." Feeling the burden lifted off her shoulders, Hannah giggled as her body untensed. Jimmy's tone turned somber as he continued, "I'm sorry that you lost your father. It's rough. I get it. I already lost both my parents. My dad, most recently."

Feeling the same painstaking connection, Hannah silently grieved with him. "I'm sorry for your loss. May I ask how?"

"Heart attack," he simply put it. "He was a tad overweight, or so he would say. Heart problems ran in his family, and he struggled with high blood pressure for as long as I can remember. I don't think he got over his wife's passing. She passed away from leukemia when I was around six. Thankfully, I don't recall seeing her suffer too much. Dad told me it was awful. I never knew my dad to cry, but I often found him crying in his room at night. Even years after she left us." The room's atmosphere did a complete one-eighty to a cold lonely place, full of despair and anguish. Her heart ached for his loss and mourning. She believed it was difficult to go on without her father in her life. Despite the distance between them for a while, she couldn't imagine even losing her mother. Alone in this world. Clearing his throat, he piped up, "So you're from New York. I have never been there. I bet it will be a blast going back. More to do around there than here." He held out his arms in exaggeration.

Hannah forced herself to laugh to get out of her stupor. "Thanks. It's very..."—she rolled her eyes playfully as if she was toying with the right word to describe the scenery—"different." She thought back to what her mother disclosed earlier. Were her school plans going to oust him if he planned to take it further? Was he only cheerful and friendly as a precursor to the goodbye once he left that evening? Even if he said he would stick it through until she completed the semester, would he indeed be there in solace? Was their relationship doomed like hers and Greg's? Her mind switched over to her ex. She forgot about his current status and her many conversations with Beth. What if she ran into Greg while she returned to school? What would she say? What would she do? What if he was still single? What if Beth did talk to him behind her back? Her head began to spin with all the questions attacking her kamikaze style. From what she knew of long-distance relationships, they didn't work out. Only a small percentage survived.

"Hey, be thankful," he teased. "You're smart, Hannah." That same handsome smile tossed her way again. "You don't want to be stuck here in some blue-collar job like me." She couldn't tell by his declarative statement if he was trying to hint at their differences or simply leaning more into the conversation.

The rest of the evening was small talk. Delilah pretty much led the conversation about her home tour and Hannah's time so far in the small town of Wapakoneta. As the evening grew into night, Jimmy politely began to excuse himself from their place in the living room and made his way to the door. Hannah's heart thumped rapidly in her chest as she practically dashed after him. "Here, I'll walk you out." She couldn't lock her eyes back on her mother. She didn't want to see the worry stretch out across her brow.

Shivering, Hannah hugged herself as the night's cold temperature caressed her skin. Jimmy took note of this and paused at the porch's stoop. "You better get back inside."

Her feet remained firm on the concrete porch underneath her. She didn't want Jimmy to leave but knew it was growing later in the night. "When I do go back to New York, you are welcome to visit. I could show you around."

"I don't think I would fit in," he chortled as he glanced down at his appearance. "I'm pretty sure I would stick out."

"Hey, I was the same way when I came here." Her eyes deviated around at her surroundings in a playful tone, with a grin. "I think I'm surviving."

"You are doing decent," he chuckled. "You still stick out."

"Is that a bad thing?" she cooed.

"No." He shook his head with a smirk. "You caught my attention."

"Not scared you away, huh?"

The smirk never left him. "Not a bit. Why? I hoped I could see you again."

Hannah bit her lip at the comment, and she nodded her head way too eagerly. "Me too."

"Next weekend? Before you leave for a bit?" He stopped. "Unless it's going to be crazy with packing. I get it."

"No, I'm good. I would love to see you."

"Well, see you then." He hesitated after he finished the sentence, then leaned over and gently pressed his lips on the right side of her facial cheek. She could feel his warm breath up against her skin, and she shivered from the sensation. His musky cologne was intoxicating. "Text me later?" His mouth inches from her ear before he pulled back.

"Yeah. Drive safe," her voice trembled as she chewed her lip again, watching him step off the porch and head to his truck. Her mind felt like she was in a drunken stupor as she turned on her heel to enter the house once more.

Delilah was waiting edgily on the couch for the newsbreak. "Well?" A cheesy grin coated all over her face.

"He wants to see me again," she announced as she walked back over.

"That's it?" Her mother sounded almost disappointed in the news, moving over to allow her daughter to sit beside her.

Hannah couldn't withhold the good news. "He kissed me on the cheek!"

March 22

"This is your captain. We are beginning our approach to La Guardia. Please adhere to the seatbelt sign and turn off any electronic devices. We should be arriving in twenty minutes. All crew members, begin the final prep." The pilot's announcement started to dim outside Hannah's earbuds before she slipped them off to hear him.

Stashing her cell back into her purse, she scooted an inch from side to side in her seat to get comfortable. She heard several oohs and awes from fellow passengers as they gaped outside their small windows to bask in the trademark towering skyline coming into full view. The city's panoply image whetted the tourists' appetites for excitement as they embarked on their vacation. Some commuters accustomed to Manhattan and its surrounding burbs did give the desired view a second as they fished for their carry-ons to stow away their laptops and tablets. This wasn't the first time that Hannah flew back to New York. Many of her family vacations were by plane. Her first flight was when she was around six, and she marveled at its splendor in a boastful manner. Still, this time held a mirrored meaning—a reversal. A warmth of normalcy begged a soft smile on her lips as she glanced to the side to see the towering famous Empire State Building and Chrysler Building. The shape of the island was outlined by its surrounding three rivers and the Atlantic. The airliner jostled slightly as turbulence bounced the plane and then she could hear the whirring as the landing gear deployed, and the flaps helped the plane decrease its speed and altitude. She could see the wing near her window lift slightly as the plane turned to continue its flight path. The city became larger and larger into view. Eagerness made her grip the arms of her chair as she pressed her head back against the cloth in the back. This was it. She was finally going home.

Beth's recognizable short red hair grabbed her attention as she trudged through the terminal gate, with her rolling luggage bag behind her. She slightly shifted her shoulder to compensate for the dueling carry-on bag that housed her hygienic products and purse. "Hannah!" Her friend's raised arm waved frantically to seek her already-fetched attention. Quickening her pace, Hannah skirted around the large airport's hustling and bustling crowd to get over to her friend, who sidestepped to allow weary travelers passage. Embracing her friend, Hannah was relieved to stop and maneuver the purse's strap once more as her friend offered to take her other bag from her burden. "Oh my god, girl! It's been forever!"

"Yeah. Thanks for meeting me here." Hannah was champing at the bit to get into the city. It beckoned to her like a far-off siren. Standing there in the sea of travelers felt awkward, and her heart skipped in her chest.

"I can't wait to let you see the place and then we need to catch up totally! I want to hear everything!" Beth motioned her to follow behind her as she navigated through the oncoming ped traffic, zig-zagging to avoid collisions. Hannah followed her lead, allowing her eyes to pan to her right to catch one final glimpse of the welcoming New York City skyline.

A couple of hours later, after the quick tour around the studio apartment that Beth had in Brooklyn, the pair found themselves finishing the evening off with some Mexican food and mixed drinks at a local cantina. Hannah playfully swirled the kabob stick that pierced a slice of strawberry and orange through the frozen red beverage in front of her. A strawberry margarita topped the night off perfectly. Beth's studio had plenty of room for an extra full-size bed, and the pair had no problems sharing everything else. Heck, compared to a dorm, the studio was more than enough space for her to live in during the fall semester. The area was far noisier in comparison to her mother's small town in Ohio. Their topics started with her mother, rebuilding her relationship with her, and then switching over to their schedules. Hannah's plan was to speak with the college registrar the following day. She already had an appointment lined up and then she would walk across campus to the bookstore to see what she could take. Beth agreed to keep her supplies at the apartment until her return. She didn't have the room in her luggage to fly them back with her, and she wasn't about to pay another price for an extra carry-on. Her stomach was packed with two carnitas and rice. Now she just wanted to sit and sip on the rest of the remnants of her margarita. Her second one for the night. Her self-imposed limit.

"Oh!" Beth's voice sparkled to life as she broke the several seconds of silence between them. "I know you are super busy tomorrow, but you need to meet me at the quad around noon, right when I get out of class."

"Why?" Hannah could sense the devilish nonrevealing, invisible smirk on her friend's face.

"There's a hottie in my class. Derrick. Black hair and—" She paused to fan herself in exaggeration. "One tight cute butt."

Hannah busted out in laughter. "And you got his number, I hope?"

Her friend shook her head. "Not yet. I have been working myself up. You know, giving him the hints." She batted her eyes, then she stopped. "I'm sure I can find one for you."

Guilt hit her, and she cringed at the proclamation. "That's okay, I'm seeing someone." Her mind flashed back to Jimmy.

Deadpanned, her friend cocked a judging eyebrow her way. She crossed her arms in displeasure. "You holding out on me? You know I need details! Looks? Butt?"

Hannah blushed at the questions. "He's good-looking." She shifted her body uncomfortably in her seat and took a long sip of her drink, feeling the alcohol hit her head.

"That's it?" Her friend almost sounded insulted. "Is he on campus?"

"No." Hannah shook her head. "He's not here."

Beth nodded her head in admiration. "Impressive, girl. OSU?"

Embarrassed, Hannah remained tight-lipped on responding. Why did she feel ashamed all of a sudden that she could not simply state that Jimmy was not a college graduate or a college attendee? She didn't think of him less, and yet she held her tongue. Beth picked up on this and tilted her head to the side in a state of confusion. As if she was trying to see past her friend's ruse. "Another university?" She cackled teasingly. "Come on. I won't judge the affiliation."

"Well, he's not in college," Hannah simply stated. Somewhat the truth and fully not a lie.

Beth's hunger was not quenched. She sat there starstruck for a few seconds and then smirked widely. "Damn, girl. An older man? I love it! Grad? A doctor?" She tapped her chin to ponder more. Her eyes lit up joyously. "Lawyer?"

Hannah shook her head by the grabs. "No." Her tone became defensive. "He didn't go to college, and he works in a factory. He works hard."

Beth's face changed to a more serious tone. She cleared her throat and took another sip of the margarita in front of her. "Oh…"

"Why does it matter?" Hannah furrowed her brow painfully at her friend's accurate reaction.

"It doesn't." Beth tried to atone for her response. "He's good in bed, right?" When her friend didn't say anything back, she gaped at her. "Girl, you need to stop holding out."

"Hey," Hannah swatted her, pressing away lightly. "I don't need a man every hour like you."

"True." Beth nodded her head in appreciation. "It gets me through life. You are missing out." Pushing her empty glass away, she sighed happily. "So…" Her words lingered in the air for a bit. "I guess that's a no to Greg now? Damn, I'm glad I didn't, you know, pull the trigger or anything, like hook you up."

Hannah shook her head fervently with a set mind. "No, I'm so over him. I probably won't see him tomorrow."

Her friend gazed her way with the last chance of hope and reconsolidation. "Unless he's looking for you. I told him you were flying in."

"You did?"

"Yeah, but he didn't believe me. I thought I was very convincing."

The trouble hit Hannah with unsettling nerves. The sheer notion of seeing Greg threw her off. She wasn't expecting it at all. "Just how much did you tell him?"

"Well, you told me your plans earlier, so I told him you might be hanging around campus for a bit." Beth detected the worry on her best friend's face in front of her. "Hey, it's a large campus. The chance is slim unless he was trying to find you."

With that, Hannah finished off her drink.

March 23

The frosty white snowflakes gently kissed Hannah's skin as she stepped out from the registrar's office's leading set of doors to embrace the frigid temperatures. The weather app on her phone stated that the temperature that day was around thirty-two degrees Fahrenheit with a ten-degree chill factor. Her bones ached inside her flesh. The session with her academic advisor was much quicker than planned. Beth's class would let out in thirty minutes, and the pair were to meet up outside the campus's book store. Hanna thought for sure that Beth would beat her there. Folding the paper up with her class schedule outlined, she placed it in her hoodie pocket and set off in the westward direction, toward the building that housed the class that Beth was currently attending. She would just show up in surprise. A few students were scurrying to either their dorms, to the cafeteria, or toward their upcoming class. Most of them had their heads down, scrolling their phones, with earbuds snugged into their ears, while others had their minds on other things as they passed her by. No one gave her the time of day. A coldness took her. It is not like the weather but instead, a reflection of the diversity between her old life and the one she endured over the months in Ohio's small town. Months ago, before the travesty took place, she would not think much of whoever was around her. She was pretty much the same as them. Her mind was pulled away by other things than what was around her—the sheer beauty of the campus, even in the greenery's dormant state.

"Hey, Hannah," a sharp male voice beckoned to her from behind, startling her. She nearly jumped a few inches off the ground as she quickly turned. Her eyes widened when she saw Greg standing there. His physical appearance remained the same, and he too was dressed in a hoodie. He proudly had the college's name bolded across the chest in yellow font, offsetting itself from the material's deep-purple shade. Judging by his attire, she pegged him not to be working his internship that day in the city. He held onto the bilateral straps of his laptop book bag that pressed against his chest. A feigned, friendly smile cracked through his stern look. "Beth told me you were flying in this weekend to get signed up for the fall. I didn't believe her." A sour note rang in his words.

Seeing her old lover standing feet away from her, Hannah found herself frozen in place. Her words jumbled together like a traffic gridlock inside her brain. "Hey, Greg. Yeah, I signed up for the fall. I need to finish up my degree." Her answer was honest, but she could still see the hurt in his eyes. Was he still mad about their breakup? Or was it something else?

"Thought you were so attached to your mom and the hicktown that you didn't want to come back here. At least that's what you told me," he scoffed at her hurtfully. "I guess I wasn't good enough."

Hannah sighed. This wasn't how she wanted to spend her free time before she met with her friend. "Greg, you know that isn't true. I had a lot going on."

"You did, and I think I was pretty fucking patient. You couldn't even give me the time of day."

"You moved on," Hannah shot back. "So why seek me out here? I know damn well that you didn't have to walk the same path as me."

The man in front of her was unmoved. "As I said in my previous statement, Beth told me you were coming back. I found someone that matches your description, so I wanted to confirm it myself."

She rolled her eyes at his comeback. Typical lawyer style. "Are you done with your defensive posture?" A knowing smirk moved across her soft pink lips.

He huffed by her taunt. "I don't know what the hell happened to you over these few months, but I'm glad I moved on." He snickered at a private thought. "You weren't even that good, to say the least."

Hurt by his insult, she narrowed her eyes. "Enjoy yourself then."

He proudly kept his head held high at her low blow. "I'm doing better than you. At least I have someone else. You keep your attitude up, and you will stay alone."

Her first instinct was to question where his alleged girlfriend was. Beth advised her earlier that she never saw anyone else with Greg in her run-ins with him on campus, but the school was large, and she had no clue really on his ex's schedule. Instead, she tossed back, "You sure about that?" She couldn't hide the grin on her face as she crossed her arms with self-satisfaction.

He scrunched up his face at the counter and sneered again at the notion. "A redneck?" He tried to save face and find her announcement humorous. "Good catch."

Rolling her eyes, she exhaled excessively through her nose and mouth. "Are we done here?"

"Didn't think I was keeping you."

"Hey, you stopped me. I was on my way to see Beth. Excuse me, Greg, and it was fantastic"—she paused to let her words drip with loud exaggeration—"meeting up with you," she continued. Spinning on her heel, she continued her way, not daring to look back. She thought she did reasonably well holding her own against him. Not what she expected walking into that day on campus. Her arms were draped at her sides, with her hands still clenched. Was it pure coincidence that he happened to stumble upon her that day? A small percentage rate. The odds were against her, given the large campus and the many paths one could take to their next class. She didn't know Greg's schedule that semester, so in his defense, he could have been going the same way as she was, but she knew for a fact that the majority of his classes would be on the east side, where most of the law programs were taught. Her brow creased with worry as she began to wonder if he was going to the same spot where Beth was. She would have to confront him again. There was no doubt about it. Only after walking for several minutes did she allow herself to glance behind her to see if he was trailing her. To her relief, he was gone, out of sight. Her heart still pounded in her chest from the confrontation. Where did he go? Did he make the extra trip to find her? She didn't see him till just then. Was he tailing her the whole time? A shiver moved down her spine. Greg wouldn't be that petty to stalk her. He seemed like he didn't care that much to give her that much time of day. Still, he was hurt that she was there, though months ago, she claimed that she didn't want to leave Ohio for a while. A lie. An unintended one. Looking down at her watch, she had about ten minutes left to see her friend. She couldn't wait to share.

March 23

Wasting no time, Hannah snatched her friend's arm and yanked her to the side to allow the exiting students to move on their way. The urgency in her silent plea tolled on her as her grip was a bit firmer than intended. Beth contravened her action and jerked her arm away. "What's going on?" Trepidation fueled her words.

Catching sideway looks of passersby interested in their private conversation, Hannah ushered her friend along toward the campus's bookstore: their intended destination. Silent, she chanced a glance over her shoulder to see Greg nowhere in sight. He wasn't going their way. "You're creeping me out." Beth was becoming frustrated, and she firmly dug her feet into the sidewalk's concrete to stop abruptly, nearly causing Hannah to collide with the back of her.

"I ran into Greg outside the registrar's office," she finally admitted, relaxing a little, once she accepted that they were in the clear. "I wasn't expecting that." She crossed her arms as the tension started to rise within her as she thought back to their heated exchange.

"Oh." Beth's eyes hastily diverted away from her, and she chewed her lip. She could see the distress on Hannah's face. "It wasn't a good meetup?" she tossed out casually.

Hannah shook her head from side to side. "He's such an asshole. He's still sore about me not coming in earlier to please him." Adding, with a huff, "I thought he went back to his ex."

"Maybe he missed you?" Her friend thoughtfully surmised.

Hannah rolled her eyes as she kept her arms crossed, still peeved. "Didn't sound like it. Not like I care."

"You didn't even give him a chance?"

Irked by her friend's pleas to take Greg's side, Hannah cocked an eyebrow. Everything was fitting together. Now it made perfect sense how he found her that day. Sure, it could have been a sheer coincidence, but the probability was very low—statistically, a twenty percent chance. The campus was large, and most of the law degree curriculum took place on the opposite side. Greg would have to be going out of his way ultimately to seek her out, or his path was a complete anomaly. "Did you tell him I was coming here?" Her tone was accusatory.

Beth fidgeted as she shoved her hands in her pockets to try to avoid direct contact with her friend. The curtain drawn to reveal the betrayal, with the spotlight on Beth at center stage. Her nonresponse confirmed the guilt. Hannah groaned. "Beth, what did you say?"

Her friend found her strength, and she turned on Hannah, with her finger pointed out. "Look, I know you and Greg had a bad breakup. I know it tore you up. I saw Greg one day on campus after we talked about you flying here to see me. I told him that you were coming in. He seemed interested."

"Why did you do that?" Hannah angrily demanded. She sighed loudly as she finally unfolded her arms.

"Hey, you were the one who kept fucking asking about him!" Beth shot back defensively. "I was trying to be your friend! I texted him last night and told him you were heading to the registrar's office. I thought it would be a nice surprise." She tossed up her arms in exhaustion. "Some friend you are! I was trying to do a nice thing!"

Hannah gritted her teeth at the predicament she was placed in. She couldn't argue the fact that Beth was trying to help her out, but still. "I told you about Jimmy. I'm seeing him now." Stopping in midsentence, she thought back to Greg's reaction when she proudly announced that she was involved. She never mentioned Jimmy's name or background, and she mostly only admitted it to retaliate against Greg's statement that he moved on. His rage of emotions revealed that perhaps he still wasn't seeing someone else. After all, he sought her out, and not her. She was standoffish at the beginning of their encounter.

Beth scoffed at her argument. "Come on, Hannah. Seriously? I know you miss the attention. Hell, I would too. Greg seems pretty still interested. Give him another chance." Her tone quieting as her latter sentence was more of a soft plea.

Feeling cornered, Hannah stood solid in place as she looked over at the bookstore that was in view. Her entire mood deflated, and the interest to prep for the fall semester just dissipated along with it. "Look, maybe it was a bad idea to come here." Her words broke free from her mouth before she had a chance to ponder their repercussions.

Hurt, Beth glared at her. "So, what? You want to leave now back to Ohio?" She held her hands on her hips. "Pfft, what about my apartment? Are you just done with me now too?"

It was hard for her to regain composure as she stood there. She needed to escape the current pressures. It was hard to tell what other words would be tossed back and forth the longer she lingered there. "Beth, you're still my friend," she confirmed. "I just need to take my mind off things." Pivoting on her heel, she turned away to head out. "I'll see you this evening back at your place." Not bothering for an acknowledgment, she quickly allowed her feet to guide her along the path. One of the many good things about attending a college in New York City, there were many places she could go to escape reality.

The N Line jolted the subway cart as it stopped at its next destination, Forty-Second Times Square. Glancing up from her phone, Hannah popped in her earbuds and followed the debarking passengers, skirting around a few that stopped to check their bearings. The terminal was more crowded than the one she departed from near her college. Times Square was a known hot spot for a tourist destination and a line interchange. Many passengers raced across the hub to their awaiting line before it left them. Some shoved past the busied tourists, bumping into a few without apology. Hannah ignored the regularity and made her way over to the escalator. It led her to the upper level and the sea of people outside. Those from the tristate area made it a common practice to avoid midtown, notably Times

Square. Those visiting clambered to that section of the island first. Those that purposefully went there were hastily wanting to capture their iconic photographs of the flashy lights and selfies, while others frequented the souvenir shops paralleling the streets. The pathways were crammed with food vendors, double-decker bus or helicopter rides tours reps, and Broadway ticket sellers. One could get a good deal on seeing a well-known show if one were lucky. Everyone outside the vendors was targeted to be tourists, and the sellers would try to flag their attention. A few minutes after their spiel, a hopeful purchase. Between this and the constant stopping ped traffic for photos made most from the metropolitan area avoid Times Square.

Before the turmoil that violently changed her life, Hannah would be like everyone else and not even come here unless she wanted to see a show. She would catch a metro ride over to Central Park to find a secluded area to find solitude for a quick lunch or study. If she felt adventurous, she would head down to Fifth Avenue to do some window shopping between classes whenever she had some free time. Today, those common points of interest eluded her. She was drawn to Times Square. Today, for once in her life, she would be the outsider. Moving her feet along, she finally paused when she reached the famous photographic section of midtown. Navigating her phone from the music app she had open to her camera, she snapped a quick photo. Her fingers then raced along the screen to send the captured image to Jimmy, ending the message with "Wish you were here." She needed to know. She needed to know what other metamorphoses her life would take in the days to come. Sure, her relationship with the blue-collar worker in Ohio was new and nowhere close to a serious tone, but would they work down the road? She was already promised a career with her father's old firm once she passed the bar. A guaranteed position was nothing to take lightly or forbode. Jimmy may have his responsibilities where he currently resided. Would their relationship fizzle out once she dug into the fall semester? She thought back to her heated exchange with Greg and her argument with Beth. Maybe her friend was right. Maybe she was lonely and needed companionship. Jimmy was very sincere and good-looking.

He was a noncollege graduate that was slaving away in a factory job. Did it even matter? If they got serious, would he make the sacrifice to leave everything he had to live in the bustling metropolis? A far cry from the rows of corn and soybean fields in Wapakoneta. Could he adapt? What if he wanted her to be the one to change their plans? What kind of career could she possibly get with her law degree in a small community town? If neither gave in, would their relationship die out just like her parents'? The message was delivered but not read yet. Tucking her phone back in her coat pocket, she returned to her low-volume chill music that streamed through her ear pods and joined in with the crowd.

Catching a young girl posing crazily with her mother for a selfie in front of the Naked Cowboy made Hannah giggle with laughter. Her heart beamed as she looked on. Hannah missed her mother and the days when joy filled her life. On the weekends, a promised trip into the city made her elementary and middle school weeks go by quickly. Love and hope filled those days. Despair entered her mind with the grim remembrance that those days were gone and no longer achievable. Her dad was lost, and her mother was in Ohio. Their house was sold, and now, besides the university, she had no ties with the city. Like the mother and daughter who were making the best of their day, she was an outsider looking in.

A glimmer of reprieve grabbed her attention when a soft chime interrupted her music to announce an incoming text. Taking out her phone, she scrolled through her messages and saw an unread reply from Jimmy. His words were short, but they were still enough to make her sigh happily to herself—a light at the end of her tunnel. "Would love to see that place. I hope you are having fun and can't wait to see you when you get back."

Her demeanor when entering the apartment that evening after dark was more at ease than earlier that day on campus. She heard her keys hanging from the keychains chime against one another as she opened the door. Beth was sitting on the couch, with a bowl of ramen noodles in her hands. She looked up with a weak wave, the best she could while holding the bowl. Setting her stuff down on a small table to her left that was used as a catching place, she walked over to where her friend sat, overhearing the evening news report from the forty-two-inch television screen in front of them. "Didn't think you would come back." Beth's words were short. She wiggled a little back in her seat and then sipped at her noodles.

"Midtown traffic. I almost forgot how busy Times Square was," Hannah admitted her whereabouts as she sat down on the other end of the plush couch.

"Wow, you must be really out of it if you went there." Beth's lament was truthful. She finally broke her serious tone with a lifted eyebrow her way. "Naked Cowboy?"

Hannah giggled. "Yeah, he was there, but not the reason."

"Man, he has to be cold. It's like twenty out there, with wind." Her friend shook her head in amusement.

"It's been forever since I went there. I'm a tourist now, so what the hell?" Hannah's nestled back against the couch and took out her cell again. Jimmy's message was staring up at her again, granting her tranquility. Her crutch.

Beth peeked her way with interest, picking up on her best friend's unspoken feelings. "He texted you?"

Hannah nodded her head with glee. "He says he would love to visit this place one day. I sent him a picture of Times Square."

Beth didn't stir from this. "Would he enjoy it?" Her question was skeptical.

Hannah wouldn't let her negativity cloud the air once again. "He may," she declared, deciding not to reopen old wounds that were festering. "Want to hit up some shops tomorrow before I head back?"

Her friend was silent for several seconds. Her contemplation confused Hannah. Was she going to give her the cold shoulder on her disproval of Jimmy? Why was she so hung up about Greg? She decided not to press the issue. After all, she would have to reside with her friend for several months during the fall semester. Even though it was quite possible with the campus lottery to pick up another place to stay, it may not have been as ideal as where she was now. She was already signed up and paid her deposit. The remainder of the tuition would be due in the following two months. If she jumped ship now, she would forfeit the deposit. Finally, Beth broke her silence to her relief. "Sure, I wanted to hit a few of the stores in SoHo. Want to go there?"

"Definitely, and Chinatown." Hannah smirked.

"Not Canal." Beth's words were finite.

"No black market," she jeered in agreement. "I just want some Chinese food."

"They don't have any there where you're staying at?" Hannah's friend asked with interest.

"Not the same."

"And I thought you didn't miss this place at all."

"Hey, I'm still a New Yorker," Hannah proclaimed with reverence.

Beth threw out another raised disbelieving eyebrow her way. "I don't know," her words sung teasingly. "You in Times Square is making me doubtful."

March 25

Hannah felt very curmudgeonly that night as she pulled her rollaway suitcase behind her, hearing its plastic wheels click over each piece of the airport's tile flooring. A yawn slipped through her mouth as she navigated the far less crowded terminal to meet her mother. Two delays coming back made her trip even longer, and she didn't arrive until ten that night instead of the planned seven. Her stomach ached for food as she skipped meals besides the tiny snacks she received on the planes from La Guardia to Detroit, then on to Dayton. Lake-effect snow dove down through the entire state of Ohio and Michigan, creating whiteout conditions. Each plane was delayed by an hour and a half. At least it wasn't better than flat-out canceled. She dreaded trying to find another free spot on anything back or even finding a hotel room in a mess.

Touching terra firma once again in Ohio made her spirits lift. Her steps quickened once her mother was in sight. Like a little girl seeking the comfort of her mother's arms, she embraced the woman in front of her tightly, smelling her recognizable cologne—a calming effect almost like serotonin. "Welcome home, sweetie," her mother's muffled words came across her shoulder.

Pushing against her seat, Hannah tried her best to get comfortable as her body craved sleep. They still had an hour's drive ahead before they got home. She felt terrible getting back so late with her mother having to work the following day, but the woman next to her in the driver's seat never complained. The few minutes starting in the car were quiet and awkward. The radio played very softly in the background at a nominal level. Finally, her mother broke the silence. "So how was your trip?" Her voice was perky with interest.

"Good. I think I managed to cram everything that I needed to do." Hannah yawned again.

"Still miss the old place?" Delilah's next question threw her off guard. She wasn't quite sure how to interpret it. Was she referring to her college? To their homeplace, or New York in general?

Hannah decided to go with her gut instinct. "I do. It felt different though." Her voice softened, "More so with Dad gone." She could almost make out a sparkle in Delilah's eyes in the darkened vehicle. The woman remained silent by her words. Hannah continued, "I'm not sure about all this."

"About what, honey?"

"Going back." She debated on bringing up Greg. She pretty much set the stage for him and Beth by her words and actions. The only problem was how actual her words would ring through the months back. She never really had a long-distance relationship. Not a serious one, if she would call it that. It wasn't like it would be a few months' deal, and that's it. She still had two more years before she could take her test to pass the bar. That only led to more questions.

"I'm sure you will do fine. You are brilliant, Hannah," Delilah began. "The first few weeks may be difficult, but you will get the hang of it. Robert would be so proud of you."

Hearing her dad's name made her scrunch her nose reactively. She was slightly bothered by the fact that Delilah referred to him by his name. She became tense. "Dad," she emphasized the word sharply. "He would be here to help me." Her eyes lowered as the fear of the unknown crept into the back of her mind once more. The same trouble she had when she signed back up. "Where does this lead me?"

"Come on, Hannah," her mother encouraged. "Don't doubt yourself. You just got back. You are going to pass that bar and then follow in your father's footsteps. Like you always wanted. You have the mind for it."

"Yeah, but then I will be alone." Her mind flashed to Jimmy. How would he fit into this puzzle? Would he pack his bags to tag along? It's not like she gave him an ultimatum.

"I will be here for you. You can't revolve your life around me. You are young, sweetie." Delilah reached out and gently took her hand in hers, giving it a light squeeze. "I know you are tired. Let's talk about something different. There's a church craft bazaar this coming weekend. We should go to that after service." Hannah giggled at the idea. Her mother quizzically glanced her way. "What's wrong with that?"

"Nothing," she chided. "I remember we used to hit the streets of Fifth Avenue to go on a shopping spree. Now we have reverted to craft bazaars." She laughed again. "Like a pair of old ladies."

"Hey now," her mother shot out playfully in defense. "You could invite Jimmy."

"To what?"

"The service and the craft show."

"Mom." Hannah shook her head quickly to disagree with the suggestion.

"Why not?"

"Men don't go to craft shows."

Delilah grinned knowingly. "They will if they want to spend time with you."

"I do that, and I will scare him off."

"Oh?" Her mother lifted an eyebrow at the acknowledgment. "You trying to keep him around?"

Hannah blushed. "Maybe... trying to. He missed me."

"Aw..." Her mother smiled warmly. "That's cute."

She swatted her away as she turned her head to look out the window to avoid any further discussion on the topic. "Enough, Mom." She stared at the parting clouds as a few stars were able to shine through the clear skies finally. The worse of the weather had already passed earlier that day. Even though she despised waiting on her flights, she wouldn't want to try flying in that mess. Snuggling against the car seat's fabric, she attempted the best she could to maneuver into a comfortable position to gain a few moments of rest.

Time slipped away for an unknown amount till new lights stirred her back to more of a conscious state. Flickering open her eyelids, she glanced around to see familiar images coming into the scene. She recognized a hotel building, followed by a Mexican restaurant that closed down for the night. The car deaccelerated as they approached an intersection, and Hannah shifted her body to sit forward with alacrity. The place where her bed resided was closing in. The light's now-green hue spanned down over the road, reflecting off the hood of their SUV, and Delilah resumed her foot position on the accelerator. Suddenly, a motion caught Hannah's peripheral vision as her mother's focus was on the road straight ahead. She turned to the left to see a maroon-colored minivan racing toward them at a high-speed rate. Its headlights were menacingly bearing down on them. Hannah opened her mouth to scream to grab her mother's attention as her entire body tensed in reaction. Delilah turned her head just in time as the vehicle was ten feet away. The last two words froze time. "Oh god." Hannah's world violently slammed into darkness.

March 25

A cacophony of garbled voices and loud engines brought Hannah back out of her unconscious state. Dazed, she groaned and quickly shut her eyes tight as a bright light hit her retinas, causing intense throbbing inside her head. Her ears were still ringing, and she felt like she was in a tunnel. A wave of nausea swarmed over here and eased after the suppression from the light intruder. "Miss, miss!" She felt a gentle tap on her arm and a woman's voice beckoning her. "Stay with me."

Slowly reopening her eyes, she was thankful to see the beam had moved away from her. All she could see was the starry blackened sky above her, and hear a mixture of radio frequencies inharmonic of one another. Her face and head stung, and when she reached to figure out the pain sensation, her arms wouldn't budge. Confused, she attempted the task again, but once again met with resistance. Her hands were restrained! "What's going on?" her voice elevated with alarm.

The woman's face now came into her view. It was an African American woman, most likely in her late thirties. "Miss, don't move. You have to remain calm." Her voice firm yet gentle at the same time. Her latex-gloved fingers were resting on her forehead, producing a tranquil state. "My name is Christine, and I'm one of the paramedics. You were in a pretty bad car accident, and we are going to transport you to be checked out."

As she listened, Hannah's mind flashed with the missing link that shored up her confusion about her current predicament. It was coming back to her! They were proceeding through the intersection when the other car came right at them. She could hear her mom's reaction and then it all faded to black. Her mom! Where was her mom? Breaking her silence with Christine, she jerked at her restraints again. "My mom! Is she okay?" Her heart was bleeding for knowledge and fear of the unknown. Where was her mom at? Her breathing became more laborious as the chance of her now no longer being in her life like her dad came into view.

"They are still working on extracting your mom from the vehicle, miss. You need to focus on yourself and stay calm," the paramedic urged more sternly.

Hannah would not hear of it. She tried to shake her head, but the collar around her neck prohibited it. "I need to see her. I want to stay here. I want to know that she is okay."

"We inbound?" A male tech grabbed Christine's attention from the current conversation. The woman lifted her head to glance at the man's way of addressing him.

"Yes, we can queue up vitals in transport. Lift on three." Christine moved to the foot of the roller as the man took position, now near Hannah's head.

She felt helpless as she looked up to see the man more clearly. He was Caucasian and appeared to be older. She really couldn't see what color of hair he had in the dark. She heard him grunt some as the roller lifted as they locked the wheels under. "Wait!" she pleaded.

The workers seemed to ignore her request as they hoisted her into the back of the awaiting ambulance. Once she was secure, the man jumped out and shut the doors to lock them in. Now she was alone with Christine. Imprisoned, Hannah felt hot tears stroll down her face. Why wouldn't they keep her with her mother? She felt like a lost child being taken away. "Shhh." Christine took to her side again. "Your mother would want you not to worry about her and focus on you. You need to calm down."

"You don't understand," Hannah choked through the flood of emotions. She was hysterical. "I already lost my father. I can't lose my mother!"

The woman was taken back by this confession, and she remained still. "I'm so sorry for your loss. I do know that your mother was conscious and responding to the firefighters on the scene. She is alive, and as soon as they get her out, she will be coming with you." A beat. "Now I need to work on your vitals and ask a few questions for triage." She swiveled around where she sat to key up the laptop to her right, anchored down to a stand. "Can you recall your name?"

"Hannah. Hannah Marks," she whimpered as she regained stability. The news was more uplifting than she assumed.

"Good," Christine cheered softly. "What is your mother's name?"

"Delilah Marks."

"Do you remember what happened?"

"Just that a car came right at us and then I can't remember anything after that." The adrenaline rush fled her body, and without the body's natural chemical masking her pain, she winced as the injuries to her body were becoming apparent to her.

Christine took note of her flinching. "Exhibiting pain?"

"This is unit two, inbound with lights and sirens. ETA thirty minutes in route," the other paramedic behind the steering wheel in the front stated over the radio that momentarily paused their exchange.

Hannah tried to look his way. Christine continued, "That is Samuel. He will get us there without issue. I promise." She returned her full attention away from the laptop and began to slip on a pair of blue latex gloves. "I'm going to palpate some areas and do a brief exam. Please let me know if you feel any discomfort or pain." She first touched Hannah's forehead and moved her eyes around to look at all angles that she could, with the collar in place. "You have an abrasion on your face. Most likely, airbag burns from their deployment and a contusion to your right cranial area. Do you recall if your head hit anything like the door?"

"I have no idea. I can't remember."

"Witnesses did advise that you had a momentary loss of consciousness. I would guess less than five minutes. That would be consistent with the hematoma and the disorientation. Any light sensitivity or nausea?"

Hannah nodded her head quickly, remembering the light intruder when she first came to her senses. "Am I going to be okay?" her voice quivered.

"Of course." Christine smiled down at her. "Remain positive." She gently pressed around her collarbones then each of her arms.

As her hands moved down her right side, Hannah gasped as a shooting pain hit her sharply. "Ah!"

Christine paused and then lightly felt around the affected area. "Hmm, possible fracture of ribs on that side."

"Fracture?" Not the news she wanted to hear!

"They can do an x-ray at the ER, to be certain," she continued until she was at her feet. Thankfully, no bouts of pain came across. Christine worked away at her laptop to note her findings.

Hannah sat quietly and then thought back to Jimmy. She was supposed to text him when they got home. What would he think if she didn't text him soon or in the next day or two? Just how long would they keep her. She had no clue where her stuff was. Was it all destroyed? Along with her phone? "Christine," she timidly called to the worker.

"Yes, Hannah?"

"My things, were they destroyed?"

"No." Christine got up and cautiously moved to the back of the unit as it traveled along in haste. She lifted a clear plastic bag that contained her purse. "We collected your purse, and the ER nursing staff will hold it for safekeeping until you are cleared or admitted."

"Admitted?"

"That would be up to the ER doctor's prognosis." She grinned at her lightheartedly. "He has the intellect. Child, I wouldn't want to do what they do." This stirred a brief giggle in Hannah, and then she flinched from the pain. Christine frowned. "Sorry."

"Is my phone all right?" She felt sorry for asking and worried if the woman would wonder where her question was leading to. Was she like a silly teenager and dying to post on social media? She hurriedly continued to not lead her this way, "I want to see if you can send a quick text to someone, to let him know where I'm going. Mom and I just got back from the airport."

Warmly holding up her hand to stop any further explanation, Christine slipped off her gloves to retrieve the desired item. "Boyfriend?" Hannah blushed. "Name?"

"Jimmy. He's in my contacts. Just tell him where I'm going," her voice trailed off as fear plagued her mind again about her mother. She prayed silently that she would be okay. She didn't want to be an orphan. A pariah. Abandoned. Not this young. No way she could adapt to facing the world alone. She needed her mother. Now more than ever. She needed her.

March 26

Throbbing pain in her hand stirred Hannah awake. She moved her arms, and the throbbing of her hand manifested into an unforgiving restrictive ache. Startled as she didn't recognize the texture of the white blanket's fabric over her legs, nor the fuzzy image of her scenery as her vision cleared up from her awakening, she nearly bolted up from her declined position into a more erect posture.

As if he transported out of thin air like something from a sci-fi television series, Jimmy was at her side, taking her nonaching hand, cupping his other hand over it. "Easy, easy," he hushed gently.

With her heart clambering inside her chest cavity, Hannah desperately held onto his hand with her own that throbbed from the IV placed in the top of the backside. She flinched as she ignored the pain. A vortex of vertigo and nausea clutched her, and she took several deep breaths to divert the sensation. The adrenaline from the shock of her predicament began to wear off, and the inhalations sparked a new spike in pain from her rib area. She winced horribly and grasped at her side, trying to ease her breaths to subdue it. His presence added more mystery to her location. Where was she? As she looked around, ignoring his concerned stare, she picked up the layout of a hospital. She was not in a private room, and only a curtain hid their location. Elevated shouts and talks could be heard everywhere outside the veil, along with beeps and alarms. Her memory found its way back. She was transported to the hospital. She remembered them rolling her from triage to radiology to perform several diagnostics of the areas of concern and then brought her there. The IV drip containing a cocktail of pain medication mixed with her drive and trip's exhaustion caused her to lose herself in much-needed sleep. She had no clue about how long she was there or when Jimmy arrived. Then she realized one person was missing from the picture. "Mom!" she gasped out. "Where's mom?"

"Easy, Hannah," Jimmy urged her. "I'm sure she's fine and still being checked out."

Hannah shook her head. The accident played back in her mind as if it was recorded. She saw the bright lights shining right into their windows, aiming right at her mother. She remembered Christine telling her that they were still working on getting her mother out of the car. That was the only status. No one told her any updates before she lost consciousness again. "Mom...," she choked as she sobbed. Tears began to flow uncontrollably as the unthinkable haunted her mind like an apparition. Why were there no updates? Someone had to know something. Were they purposefully hiding information from her until she was on the mend? Anger tousled its way inside her mind. How could they? Where was the humanity? Would Jimmy be so low to conspire with them? She shook as her nerves were overloaded with worry and doubt. Chimes started to blare from the equipment linked with the wireless electrodes on her body to monitor her heart rate as it began to escalate. "She's dead, I know it." She sobbed over and over uncontrollably, ignoring the warning. Why was God so cruel in taking not just one parent from her but two? What plan was that?

Jimmy leaned in closer to where he stroked her hand with his thumb to try to ease her. "Shh..." He breathed into her ear as he gingerly tried his best to hold her, avoiding any further cause of pain to her. "Don't think like that." Hannah buried her face into his shoulder as she continued to cry in mourning. He removed his hands and stroked her hair as he kissed the top of her forehead. "Stay here. I'll grab a nurse and see if we can get answers. Just stay calm. Okay?" His loving eyes lingered for some sort of acknowledgment. A silent, timid nod was the best she could entertain before he slipped away behind the curtain. She sat still and tried to listen as best as she could for the conversation, but the emergency room din depleted all hope of that. She had to remain there, hopeless. Minutes later, which felt like an eternity for her, Jimmy reappeared with a hopeful look. "I went to the nurses' station. They are going to have the ER doctor on call come here to provide status." Hannah nodded her head somberly. Hannah sat there, refusing to lay back down, waiting. Jimmy sat down in the chair next to her bedside and gave her the time she needed to get her thoughts together. "It will be okay," he finally broke the silence as if he was reading her mind.

Trying to change her mind's thoughts, Hannah wiped her face with her hands. "I hate for you to see me like this." After all, she was sitting in the bed, practically naked. The hospital gowns tied around the back, and indeed, hers was not properly tied. She clutched the blanket to provide some clothing the best she could. "I must look awful." She tried to look her best when she met up with Jimmy: glamorous and attractive. A troubled woman with a hospital gown and an IV stuck in her hand was nowhere on that list.

Jimmy chuckled with a cracked smile as he leaned over across the rail and held her fingertips with his hand. "Not at all. I wouldn't want to be anywhere else with you like this." Hannah blushed. He squeezed gently and continued, "After all, I sped like crazy to just get here."

"You didn't have to do that."

"Yes, I did. Hannah,"—his voice in a more serious undertone—"I love you."

The drawn curtain pulled away her attention as a man in his upper fifties, with a white coat, entered their private conversation created a rapid silence. He turned only slightly to return the curtain to its original position to complete what privacy he could in the chaotic emergency room. His brown eyes glued to the tablet in front of him. His hair was a sandy color, and a pair of bifocals were fixed upon his nasal bridge. "Ms. Marks?" He glanced only slightly for an acknowledgment before scrolling with his finger on the tablet screen. "I am Dr. Shepard, the ER physician on duty. How are you feeling?"

"I'm okay." Her mouth felt dry in her response as her instinct was to implore him for some status on her mother. She quickly withdrew her hands from Jimmy as anxiety hit her. She tried her best to keep it inside, embarrassed to let it show in front of them. Her hands twirling with the bed sheet to seek some personal comfort. The remainder of her words wouldn't budge in her throat as if concrete encased them.

Finally, giving her his utmost attention, a warm smile spread across his lips in assurance. "I looked over your chart. Your CT of your head was unremarkable. No suspect white matter to be concerning and no mass effect. The x-ray of your chest revealed one nondisplaced fractured rib." He moved over to a box of supplies on a table and retrieved a pair of bright-blue latex gloves, slipping them on. Without another word, he approached her and gingerly turned her head to the left to inspect the right side of her face. His fingertips gently touched her skin right below the hairline. "Is that tender?"

"A little, but not too bad."

He remained quiet for several moments before stepping back, discarding the gloves. "Based upon everything that I see, I believe you sustained a mild concussion. The hematoma on your face does confirm impact, and the EMS did report a brief loss of consciousness with mild photophobia. No amnesia, so that is good. Your Glasgow coma scale is fifteen, so another positive note. The rib fracture should heal on its own without any intervention. I will recommend that they keep you here for twenty-four hours, just for observation of the concussion. Upon discharge, I will recommend that you follow up with your family doctor and an orthopedic regarding the fracture. If you should exhibit any further symptoms related to the concussion, please see a neurologist. I will send paperwork to discuss how to treat for all at home and recommend thirty-six hours of brain rest."

"And my mother?" Hannah finally found her voice as she digested everything that he was telling her about her prognosis. "Delilah Marks."

Dr. Shepard appeared confused by her unpredicted question, but then he returned to his tablet. His fingers swiped the screen a few times to the right, and then his index finger tapped away. Most likely, he was plugging in her name to do a query search. She allowed him time to review the results as she gave a worried glance over at

Jimmy. The silence seemed to drag on for an eternity, and fear of the worse encroached in. "Oh, thank you for reminding me," Dr. Shepard finally answered. "Your mother is currently at the OR to be prepped for internal fixation of her left wrist. She sustained a moderately displaced fracture of her ulna. Our ortho saw her, who advised that surgical intervention was necessary."

"Oh god," Hannah gasped at the first piece of information as tears filled her eyes, and her hands rose to her mouth.

"She also sustained two rib fractures on the left. One was displaced, which created a pneumothorax. We had to place in a chest tube to drain the blood from the lung, but the case was mild, and the tube won't have to stay in for too long. We plan to keep her admitted for several days until she can be cleared. Her orthopedic will follow up after the surgery here, and then our physical therapy staff will see her. I will also recommend a pulmonologist to clear the chest tube." He tapped a few screens to make notes on the file.

All she could do was sit there and cry at the news. Jimmy moved in and gently held her as best as he could with the bed rail and her IV in place. "Will Hannah be able to see her?" he pressed, picking up the conversation.

"Of course. Once she's in recovery, a room will be assigned to her. The nursing staff can give you the details upon discharge."

Jimmy glanced back at Hannah for any follow-up. She shook her head somberly as she tried her best to hold herself together. The news wasn't as grim as feared, and yet there was still disdain in her heart that she couldn't fathom at the very second. She needed time to gather herself and harness whatever strength she had left. The path ahead for them would be rough, but they went through more challenging times and endured. They could make it through. She would be at her mother's side. Despite the anguish and hatred she had in her heart for years toward the woman currently in the OR, she would not abandon her. Her mother needed her daughter, and Hannah would answer the call.

March 27

Still with her ID bracelet around her wrist, Hannah paced in circles in the small dark-lit waiting room outside the ICU ward. She was discharged two hours ago the following day and made a direct beeline to her mother's known location. The nurse on duty advised that her mother had a successful operation. However, she was still in ICU because of pneumothorax. They wanted to keep her under tight surveillance to make sure pneumonia didn't settle in. Her wrist was pinned and stabilized. Gingerly propping one hand upon her side to nurse her rib injury, she winced in pain. Her medication was wearing off, and it wasn't about time to be due for another pill. She began to wonder if their misfortune was how God intended to make her atone for the way she treated her mother over the years. The ramification was justified. She despised her mother and ignored the woman's every effort to maintain her bond with her daughter, her only child. Hatred seeped in like an infection and spread like wildfire throughout her being. As the years progressed, she loathed Delilah and made every effort not to communicate unless her father urged or pleaded with her. Her schoolwork gave her a great excuse to say she was too busy to stay in contact, and she would go weeks, then months, without any response. At first, she didn't care if her mother was out of her life for good. Yet fate brought her outside in a despairing waiting room, yearning to be at her bedside.

A gentle tap on her shoulder made her stop in her march to see Jimmy motioning to the black adjustable watchband on his left wrist. The digitalized numbers displayed "6:00." The ICU visitation hours were now in effect, and she hurried toward the door just as more worried loved ones rose from their seats. Pausing just outside the door, she felt herself grow red in the cheeks when she realized that she left Jimmy behind. Her mind was so focused on seeing her mother that she forgot about the only person in Ohio who stayed by her side for practically the last twenty hours. He did need to leave to clean up and assured her that he would rush. Fear gripped her in the isolated hospital room, but she knew she was safe. He stayed much longer than she anticipated, and she could tell in his facial expression that he wanted to remain there. A call was placed into his work shortly after her transfer out of the emergency room. He called out his subsequent shift to stay with her—another unspoken request. Slipping around the other visitors who graciously granted him a passing, Jimmy took to her side, and the two were the first to be in line to request inside the bustling ICU.

After a brief pause that followed her call to the nurses' station, the doors swung open automatically, and symphonic beeps and tones echoed throughout that particular section of the hospital. Nursing staff and doctors moved about on their tasks while, surprisingly, a female police officer was first at the station. This was Hannah's first time back in ICU, so she had no clue which secluded room her mother was in. A dry-erase board with names and numbers hung toward the back of the small, but from her position, she couldn't make out the exact details. The young male nurse talking with the officer caught her glimpse and paused. The officer caught on and politely sidestepped to give Hannah room to move in closer. Timidly, she spoke out, "Delilah Marks? I'm her daughter, Hannah," tossing out her name in hopes that the close relation would mark the particular urgency of her visit.

The nurse's green eyes widened by her statement and glanced over at the cop once more. The officer stepped back over to intervene. "Ms. Marks? I'm Lieutenant Hale. I came here in hopes of wrapping up my report. I was one of the responding officers at the scene to investigate the crash."

Déjà vu slammed into her, and she almost felt her inner being backing away. The violent death of her father displayed in her mind and the events that transpired. She clearly could recall the conversation she and her mother had with the officer on that case as well. "Yes?" Her mouth was arid.

"I was hoping that your mother would be up to speaking with me to give her statement." Her ocean blue eyes panned over to the nurse briefly as she took out a notepad and pen from one of the many compartments of her utility belt. "It sounds like she's still recovering from her surgery, so I didn't want to press the issue. I understand you were a passenger in the vehicle as well. May I speak with you?"

Hannah chewed her lip as a barricade rose to prevent her from checking in on her mother. Jimmy patted her shoulder in comfort and then stepped off to the side near the aisle's far end. His hands shoved into his pockets as he casually waited for her. "Sure."

"Can you recall anything about what happened before the crash?"

Searching her memory bank, Hannah furrowed her brow. "We were heading back from Lima. My mom started to go through this intersection and then this car just came right us on Mom's side." Her words trailed off in a hint that she needed to see her mother.

The officer nodded her head as she scribbled down a few bulletins in her notepad, picking up the details she needed. "Thanks. I hate to say it, but this kid that hit you guys didn't have insurance."

Her jaw slightly dropped from the news. The technicalities of insurance were not her forte. She knew about civil tort cases from her studies and knew the gist behind insurance purposes. "Uh, what does that mean?"

"Just file it with your insurance and advise them. They can handle it." Hale returned her notepad in its original place, and the pen, then slipped her a business card. "The report should be ready in seven days. Here's my information if you or your mother need anything. I'm sorry that this happened to you."

Tucking the card away in her pants, Hannah nodded her head in grateful appreciation. "Thank you, officer," her voice quivered.

"I wish your mom well." The officer waved farewell and proceeded to exit the ward, with her boots tapping along the porcelain tiles. Hannah could hear the doors automatically opening as she turned to retrieve Jimmy and go back to her desired task.

The male nurse was still at his station when she returned to him. "Your mom is in 3B. You can go back and see her." He warmly smiled with encouragement.

Nodding her head, she pivoted on her heel to head in the direction of the room. Jimmy gingerly slipped his fingers, interlocking with hers, and gave her a slight squeeze. "It will be okay. You got this."

She couldn't help but smile fondly at him as the pair strolled along the corridor to her mother's room. It was barely lit inside, and a blue curtain blocked their view from the glass doorway. She entered first and slowly pulled the curtain aside. Her bed's position elevated Delilah with her tray to her right side that contained a clear plastic cup with a few sips of water left along with a minor pitcher next to it. Her wrist was in a short arm cast and a sling. An IV bag placed in her left hand with its stand nearby, and a few more wires with a cerulean-blue chest tube were hooked up to another piece of machinery. The woman's head was turned away from the doorway as if she was watching whatever scenery she had from her window. Her eyes widened, and tears of joy streamed down her face when her mother saw her daughter standing in front of her. "Hannah." Delilah's arms reached out, ignoring the restraining wires bilaterally.

Moving in swiftly, Hannah leaned over and gently hugged her mother and wept. Despite Jimmy also being in the room, this was a private moment shared among them only. Together, they have endured such hardship in the past three months, but it felt like fate was dealing them another blow again. As she leaned back, Hannah grimaced as a sharp stinging pain came from her fractured rib, and she held her side to suppress it. Delilah frowned with worry. "Sweetie, please, you need to take care of yourself."

Smiling sloppily, Hannah shrugged the request off playfully. "I'll be fine. We just need to get you out of here."

Delilah held up her arms in defeat, displaying the various wires that were hooked up to her. "Be my guest."

Jimmy chuckled. "Only for your good, Ms. Marks."

Her mom's eyes twinkled with hope and wonder. "Good to see you again, Jimmy."

Hannah smiled back at him and took his hand once more in hers. "He's been at my bedside since the emergency room."

"Well." He rubbed the back of his neck. "Minus a few hours." Sparing her from the unnecessary details.

The smile on Hannah's face quickly faded when she recalled the conversation she had with the officer right before her arrival. "Mom, I bumped into the officer before I came here. She said that the other driver that hit us didn't have insurance." She patted her pants pocket. "She gave me her card and told me to reach out to her if we needed anything."

The news made the woman in the bed sigh with frustration. "My dumb luck. I guess I'll have to call the insurance company when I get out of this place."

"I got it, Ms. Marks. I'll help Hannah file a claim once we leave here. You rest," Jimmy interjected reassuringly.

Delilah basked in delight again by his sheer kindness. "Thank you, Jimmy." She sighed again as she looked down at her thin gown and her blanket-covered waist. "I must look like a mess now." A slight chuckle exited her mouth at her jab. "I'm sure the car's a total. At least we are safe and still here." Her eyes grew dark as she lowered them. "Though it would have been nice to see Robert once more."

Hannah took her mother's hand in hers once more and kissed the top of it. "You will one day, Mom." It humbled her to witness open devotion to Robert after all those years thinking that her mother didn't care about him anymore."

Defeatedly, Delilah grimly reminded her, "I guess I will be out of work for a while like this." She sighed again. "The house is such a mess. I shouldn't have put the repairs off as I did."

"I'll get a job if I have to," Hannah spoke up quickly, though she had no clue what profession she could find to match her college degree in the quaint town. The idea of doing retail was never on her list. To make ends meet, she may have to do just that. "I could see about working at your office," she tossed out enthusiastically. An office job wouldn't be too bad, and it could give her something to do while she was out of school. Some of the renovations around the house required more than one person and someone who knew what they were doing.

"Hannah." Delilah stopped her in awe, not expecting the willingness of her daughter to pick up the slack though they were in a predicament.

"I'm pretty handy, Ms. Marks," Jimmy chimed in. "I can see what I can do to help out you or Hannah." His eyes were warmly panning over to Hannah. "I can be there every day after work if I have to."

"Jimmy." Delilah shook her head. "I can't ask you to do that. I'm sure Hannah and I can manage once I'm out of here."

"Mom," Hannah urged. The notion of seeing Jimmy every day was very inviting, even if it was her plan. Plus, he may be more beneficial than she would when it came to home repairs on their renovations.

"Crap. I forgot to call into work. Let me step outside for a moment," Jimmy quickly changed the subject as he retrieved his cell from his pocket.

Concerned, Delilah followed up, "Do you need to leave?"

He shook his head and pointed to the hallway. "I'll be right back."

Hannah kept her focus on his whereabouts, even as he left the room. She was in awe of him at her side there and his willingness to assist them. How did she luck out so well? A big smile spread across her lips from her thoughts. Delilah picked up on this and beckoned her attention once more. "He's very good to you," she pointedly reminded her.

"Yeah," Hannah admitted, not turning her focus away. "You know what, Mom? I think I'm in love."

May 30

The return to church was paramount to Hannah's mom. A few days following the hospital discharge, the notion occurred in one of their daily chats. Her mother longed for it yet steered away, given what happened with the accident and her physical appearance. At that time, her arm was in a short-arm cast, and she was on the first steps of her recovery. It would require many weeks or months of rehabilitation and follow-up with an orthopedic. Her mother took the brunt of the force from the impact. With the town being a small-knit community, the violent crash was the talk of the town. Television reporters and newspaper journalists were turned away by her mother's discretion. She was not the one who revered in the limelight, especially when it came to personal gain. She didn't want sympathy. Delilah just wanted the waters to calm before venturing out into town once more to go on with her normal life. Her doctor placed her out of work so that short-term disability would help with the expenses. Jimmy graciously volunteered to do any errands after his shift at work and even offered to hang around their house to assist in cooking dinner or just keep them company. Firing up the grill was the highlight of the beginning of Hannah's summer: soon to be her last summer in her new home before heading back to New York for the fall term. She had to admit that Jimmy sure knew his stuff when it came to grilling hamburgers. She never tasted something so wonderful in years. Her mother even added a teasing elbow bump and knowing smile, hinting that their house visitor was a "keeper."

The return to church was harder on her mother than on Hannah, even though her mother was a member. Many of the congregates mailed cards filled with good wishes to them right after the accident and hoped to see them come much sooner than they did. Delilah appreciated the tokens privately but dared not to face everyone in her condition. After she transitioned from the cast to a brace, she finally took the plunge. Delilah even encouraged Hannah to invite Jimmy. Hannah obliged, and he openly accepted, but she felt very awkward in asking him. She wasn't too sure by his quick response if he was a man of faith or if he just accepted to get more time with her.

Hannah had to admit that the man was persevering. More so than the past boyfriends she had in her life. They were formally a few months into their blossoming relationship, yet it felt like they had been going steady much longer than that. Unlike most "standard" relationships, they were not on the level one would expect in that time frame. They barely reached the physical point because of her recovery, and Jimmy was the one who didn't press it. Even when she felt like she could participate in some sexual aspect, he declined. He could tell she was still mustering through all the pain. Each time it came to that point, after minutes of passionate kissing, he would squeeze her hand and tell her they would have time. Her mother's transition marked a crucial moment in Hannah's timeline too. She was fully recovered, so she wanted to make her relationship with Jimmy now more "normal." Approaching this subject would take planning and privacy and was not something one would bring up in the house of God.

Going back to religion, she and Jimmy never discussed it. Even though raised as a Catholic, she never really devoted herself to her faith and God as one would expect. There was the belief in some fashion, a fragment of what it could be, growing larger ever since her father's loss. When there was no one else to face her demons, the Lord was there and guided her. This part of her life remained under lock and key, and she felt silly to divulge it to Jimmy. He never spoke about God outright. Maybe he thought the same about that as she did?

The air-conditioning pouring through the vents inside the church's main lobby tickled Hannah's exposed legs and arms, and she shivered. Her flower spring dress flowed as she walked in step with her mother to the center of the building that housed the sanctuary. A few familiar faces greeted them with pamphlets. Delilah remained quiet. "You okay, Mom?" Hannah furrowed her brow at the woman, with worry.

Her mother nodded her head. "Yeah. Let's find our seats." Selecting the third row, Delilah sat down first with Hannah beside her. "I think Jimmy should be able to see us when he walks in."

Hannah chewed her lip at the mention of his name. They were already late getting there, and she didn't see his car in the rows of parked vehicles. Perhaps he had a change of heart? She debated going to the front door and looking for him there and then she felt bad for leaving her mother there alone. Her heart raced in her chest as she anxiously waited for his arrival. She became elated when she recognized him entering the sanctuary. He was dressed in dark denim jeans, a collared short-sleeved gray polo shirt, and shiny almond-colored dress shoes. He sidestepped to allow passersby through as his eyes eagerly combed the occupants. Hannah stood up and motioned at him with her hand, which he caught seconds later and acknowledged her with a swift nod of his head. Sitting back down, her hands trembled as she nervously removed her purse from his reserved seat and stuffed it under her chair. The recognizable scent of his aftershave poured into her nostrils and soothed her ever-beating heart. She could feel his body heat next to her as he sat down. "Sorry I'm late," he whispered to her.

"Almost," she playfully teased, with a nudge into his shoulder with her own.

Delilah leaned over to get into view and flashed the newcomer a warm smile. "Hello, Jimmy. Glad you could join us."

"Ms. Marks." He untucked the Bible he was carrying and placed it on his lap. "Thanks for the invite."

"You're always welcome," Delilah whispered lower as the band walked on the stage to strike up the worship.

Hannah felt even more nervous as she rose from her seat with the congregation to begin their praise. Jimmy took her side, very calm and collected. It was as if he did this before, or maybe this didn't bother him. She felt so giddy, like a young schoolgirl gushing over their crush. What made him like this? Her hands timidly rested on the back of the seat in front of her as her eyes stared at the lyrics. The room filled with an inspiring and delightful chorus, and it seemed to drown out her mind. As if on cue, Jimmy reached over and gently clasped her hand with his, giving a gentle squeeze. She could feel the warmth of his skin on hers; she leaned over and delicately placed her lips on his cheek.

The afternoon's fresh, warm air embraced the trio as they exited the church following the service. Hannah spotted Jimmy's truck, three aisles to the right of their space, so their paths would remain the same for a bit. She revered in it. Their hands still clasped together as they walked along. "What a beautiful day," Delilah sighed in awe. "I'm sure glad we are over the cold mess."

"I can change and head back over in two hours to finish up the paint on that one side today," Jimmy offered. He had been at their house on and off almost every weekend to focus on the most needed repairs. His help alone saved them money and lessened the time. The place looked gorgeous, and all the remodeling was done entirely the way Delilah wanted. The fresh coat of paint brightened their moods versus the tacky wallpaper. Despite her grandmother's choices being removed, it still felt like home.

"Nuh-uh," her mother surprisingly declined the gesture. "Today is your day together. Go out and have fun. You don't want an old woman tagging along."

"Mom." Hannah laughed with a playful swat at her. "You're not old."

"You are feeling better now, Hannah, and I can manage on my own."

"You sure?" Jimmy's eyes caught Hannah's with hope before he refocused his attention on the woman in front of them.

"Of course." Delilah deliberately turned to head down her aisle before the conversation could continue. "Have fun!" She called back with a wave.

"Lunch?" Jimmy offered as he led her over to his truck.

"Sure thing."

The pins' loud crack as the bowling ball collided echoed throughout the alley, followed by a discord of other striking pins in the nearby lanes. Hannah smiled as Jimmy pivoted with a gratified cheer before stepping off the ledge to sit down next to her. "Your turn." A challenging nod from his head urged her to get up from where she sat.

"Come on." She laughed as she obliged to retrieve her pick of the lime-green house ball from where it rested. "You knew what you were doing when you brought me here." She picked up her ball and wiped some of the grease off it with a cloth. "This was a complete setup."

"Course not." He shook his head playfully. "I didn't bring my ball. This was spontaneous."

His answer sparked a raised eyebrow on her face. "Your ball? I get it now. You're like a pro, right?" She pointed up to his standing score of 130 on the seventh frame, a massive gap from her pitiful sixty. Breaking one hundred was a barrier to her.

"Nah," he chuckled at her insight as he crossed his arms, relaxing back in his chair as much as he could with the hard molded plastic supporting his upper and lower lumbar. "Go ahead."

"You want to see me throw another gutter?" Hannah prodded as she turned on her heel to face the pins in front of her.

"Don't think like that."

She never thought that their day would continue past their lunch at the local family restaurant to a few bowling games. The sport never really appealed to her. She did it for fun when she was around ten, with her parents, three times the most. Never after turning twelve. Her likes evolved to fashion, and she often found herself setting out to the mall or into the city. The bowling alley was never a place to go on a date, at least not with her past boyfriends. She could almost see Greg snarking at Jimmy's choice. Realizing she was captivated by her thoughts, she threw the ball quickly. The orb thumped along down the lane, heading left before it nestled itself in the gutter and continued its course: null. Aggravated at just how bad of a player she was, she turned to await the ball's return, avoiding eye contact from her date in embarrassment. If he expected that they would revere in a fun pastime, he was gravely mistaken. His skill made her wonder. Was she his type? Scowling, she fumed silently.

"Don't give up," he called from his chair, almost reading her mind. "You can do it. Just think about it."

"So how did you get so good?" she casually asked, delaying the inevitable.

"My dad," he quickly answered. "He and I used to hit this place since I was a kid. He showed me what I know. Bowled even on a few leagues in my youth."

"Leagues?" Hannah groaned. "You are a pro."

"Nah," he dismissed her grasp with a wave of his hand, sitting up straighter. "Never hit a perfect game. You caught me in my off-season, so to speak."

"This is your off-season?" She pointed up to the score monitor once more.

The animated image on his face slowly dissipated as a more serious tone took him. "I haven't been here for years, not since Dad died. I couldn't do it."

Her stomach turned to stone as it weighed heavily. Moving over to next to him, she took his hand. "I'm sorry. This means a lot to you, huh?"

He squeezed her hand back and then chuckled. "It's okay. I know Dad watches over me. It's rough."

"I get it. It's been hard since I lost my dad. I can't even…"

"Day by day. It's been years for me, and you are still fresh in it. I get it." He leaned over and gingerly kissed her forehead. "I'm here for you. Know that." She couldn't help to smile at him as he moved away, her words lumping in her throat as tears swelled in her eyes.

"Jimmy," she finally found her voice, and her lips trembled. "I love you…"

Cupping her face with his other hand, he allowed his thumb to brush up against her soft skin. "I love you too, Hannah." Leaning over, he gently took her lips in his.

His taste was sweet and enchanting. Hannah laced her fingers together behind his neck and moved in closer, brushing the front of her body up against his. This prompted an increase in passion. A slight moan escaped his lips as his tongue moved into her mouth, searching her own. She lightly flickered his back and felt the heat of his breath up against his skin as his hands moved off her face and down her arms, sending shivers down her spine. A few more seconds into their hot embrace, and he broke away, panting. His eyes were darting nervously to the unnoticing patronages nearby. No one looked their way. "Sorry." He bashfully smiled at her. "I shouldn't have."

"It's okay." Hannah chewed her lip as her body yearned for more of him. She was ready. "I want to…" Her words trailed off, hinting at the pretense.

Nodding his head, "You sure? I mean, we can give you more time to recover. I'm not pushing you." He scooched his body inches back into his seat after realizing how much further he was on her side at the counter.

Hannah flirtatiously smirked and batted her eyelashes slowly. "Jimmy, I want you."

"Then let's pack up."

Once inside his pickup, Hannah reached into her purse to retrieve her cellphone to send a quick message to her mother. Despite her age and the state of her independence, Hannah knew her mother would worry if she didn't show back up at the house without a call or text. After all, they have been through, she couldn't blame her. Her fingers dashed across the phone's keyboard to type out the message, taking only seconds before hitting send. Her mother could easily read between the lines to understand Hannah's next step in her relationship with Jimmy. Putting her cellphone back into place, she reached over and gently took his right hand, giving it a slight squeeze. Her heart pounded rapidly in her chest like a furious drum solo at a heavy metal concert. The feeling was vexing. Why? It wasn't like she was a virgin and never had sex before. She had been naked before in front of another man and shared her body. A sin that most of the faith would shun upon. Still, the anticipated session made butterflies flutter in her stomach, like a young teenager. The touch of his thumb gently stroking the skin of her hand partially eased her nerves. "Ready to go?" He paused for her response before the vehicle into gear.

She gently leaned over and kissed him on the cheek, allowing her breath to caress his smooth-shaven face. "Absolutely."

Her eyes opened as she stirred away, beating the dawn. She shivered as she realized she was still naked in Jimmy's bed, with the sheet partially covering her up. Pulling the cover up higher, she felt the smoothness over the material caress her flesh. She turned her head to see Jimmy's back to her as he was still asleep. Smiling at his sleeping form, she turned over on her other side to face his body directly as she thought back to their encounter. They took their time just as she hoped, and their lovemaking was terrific. He was so sensual to her every need and desire. She longed to remain in bed for days without anything pressing her to move away. The sound of a distant train and a car driving down the street echoed outside as the town was starting to awaken. The birds chirped on their perches as a small ray of sunlight began to shine through the turned-down blinds. The day called her like a supernatural being. Reality bolstered through the doors of her mind, crushing whatever harmony was inside. Time did not freeze. It flourished and ventured on like the train outside.

A new day had already begun. Soon it would be time for her to pack up her bags in less than three months and head back to New York to finish up her degree. Despite the trip only lasting for about four months, the news saddened her and clouded her with worry. She built up so much in these last five months. Was it only to be knocked down like a raiding horde? Frowning, she could not prevent the unthinkable thoughts come at her. What if something horrible happened to her mother during her absence? What if God took her away so swiftly like her dad, not allowing a farewell? Could he punish her so severely in less than a year? What if another caught Jimmy's eye while she was so far away? Would he remain faithful given their relationship of only a few months? What if New York kept her there? She would have to do an internship in the spring semester, which meant staying more in the bustling city. She already had a foot in the door with her dad's firm. An excellent path was forged for her. Jimmy had many ties to Ohio, and what would he do if he stayed in New York? Were they meant to divide? Was she fated to be alone, or maybe Greg was the obvious choice?

As if he could sense the turmoil that seized her heart, Jimmy murmured sleepily and moved over on his other side to face her, with his eyes groggily looking at her. A twisted grin moved over his lips as he saw her in the bed next to him. "Good morning."

Flashing a fake smile back, she cuddled up against him and kissed his lips sweetly. "Good morning, sleepyhead."

"Sleep well?"

"Yeah…" she teased. "You wore me out."

He chuckled and maneuvered onto his back as he reached out to her with his right arm to hold her in his arms. "I did?"

She nestled his chest, allowing the soft chest hairs to tickle her skin. "You were amazing."

He gently traced his fingers up and down her arm. "I think you were better." He yawned. "What time is it?"

She rolled away briefly to check her phone. "Six-thirty."

Her response prompted him to scramble out of bed in haste, nearly tripping over the sheet that was tangled up with his body. "Shit."

"What is it?" her voice rang with alarm as she froze in place to watch him.

"Shit, shit!" He scrambled around the room, grabbing at his clothes. "I'm late for work." He stopped in midstride as he headed toward the bathroom and turned back to her. He kissed her lips. "I'll talk to you after work. There's an extra key on my nightstand. You can shower here and lock up." He stopped again, realizing she got to his place by his truck.

As if she could read his mind, she playfully pushed him away. "Don't worry, Mom can get me. Go on." With a wink, he moved to the bathroom.

June 25

Despite the thick humidity that plummeted the valley, just being outside that early afternoon was euphoric for Hannah. She and her mom spent the early morning going down to a local plant nursery to pick out flowers to spruce the barren flower bed. The once-desolate image of weeds and stem remnants of forgotten dead flowers was transformed into something more curbside appealing. Purple and pink pansies with a dash of pink splash filled the bed up. Their now-empty containers were still on the ground along with their half-empty bag of garden soil, while Hannah and Delilah took a brief water break. As the day progressed, the humidity was kicking and igniting the temperature into the more forecast ninety degrees. An early heatwave was smoldering most of the state. Summer made its grand entrance, reminding her why some disproved of the hot season. Wiping the sweat from her brow, Hannah rubbed the bottle's cool surface up against her forehead, providing some relief from Mother Nature.

"I think we did good," her mother admired their handiwork as she gulped down her water. The house was finished with all the renovations, thanks to Jimmy's assistance. Even the state of it now allured Hannah, unlike her first impression of it. It wasn't as glamorous or as big as the one on Long Island, but it was cozy, and their remodeling of the inside and out really made it feel more like home to her, despite its location not even being close to the Empire State.

"Though I think we can't compare to Jimmy," she added the last snippet playfully, jabbing at her lovesick daughter.

Hannah blushed at the mention of his name. "Hey, I think we made a dent."

Delilah mourned distantly as her eyes panned across the flower bed once more than the yard. "Robert and his flowers." She giggled at her private memory.

"Hmm?" Hannah cocked her head her way, picking up on the comment.

The warm smile on her mother's face didn't fade. "Robert always loved flowers, or at least giving them to me. Every occasion, after every fight. It was very predictable." She sighed happily. "I'm sure I received plenitude of roses throughout our marriage and even while we were dating. It was his thing, roses, white ones."

"White ones?" The color stood out since red was the predominant choice for tokens of admiration and love.

"The color choice perplexed me too. I even had to look up its meaning. I didn't know that roses' colors meant something. Heh, leave it to your father."

Hannah chewed her lip at the bit. She wanted to know herself, and her cellphone was inside the house. "What do they mean?"

"A lot of things—new beginnings, sincerity, unity." A beat. "A love stronger than death." Her voice grew still, like water in the eye of a hurricane.

Seeing the immense pain in her mother's eyes, Hannah reached out and squeezed her mother's hand comfortingly. "I remember Dad giving you flowers a lot. I always thought you liked them."

"Actually," Delilah chuckled. "I couldn't stand them. I always lectured him on spending money on something that was going to die in a few days, especially during Valentine's Day." She shook her head happily. "He wouldn't listen, or at least didn't want to." There was a slight pause, then her words turned grave. "I guess it seems like flowers didn't save our marriage either."

"Mom," Hannah coaxed her delicately, still keeping the woman's hand with her own. "It wasn't just you. Things happen for a reason." As she sat there comforting a hurt woman, Hannah realized that she never thought she would be in that position. She was caring for Delilah. The woman she blamed for the division in her family. The same woman was torn between choosing her mother over her own family. Family versus family. She took no pity upon her before. Things happen for a reason, mainly controlled by God's will. Despite turning her back on God upon the death of her father, a revelation was coming about. The pieces were coming back together, unraveled from the depth of the mystery. As she held her crying mother in her arms, nestling her chin upon the fluff of her hair, rubbing her back, an aurora bathed her. A calling from a higher power. As if a voice was speaking to her in a frequency that only she could interpret. An unknown yet familiar voice. Was it her Lord or her father from heaven? This is why things happened the way they did. This is why her father lost his life that night in December. It took the death of Robert Marks to bring Delilah and Hannah back together finally. Two suffering women who needed one another more than Hannah believed.

"Hannah, baby, I'm so sorry." Her mother's choked words caught her off guard. She recoiled from her slowly in confusion. Delilah shook her head as she pushed herself to get an unknown heavy burden from her chest. "I regret each day about how things went, missing your teenage years. Some of the important moments of your life, I missed all of it." Tears streamed down her face like tiny rivers channeling down an empty dirt bed. "You grew up so fast. I never told you how sorry I was for all this. Robert and I." A melancholy sigh escaped her mouth. "We could have worked things out. Why didn't we?" Her words echoed in the air, having a ghostly debate within.

"Mom." Hannah took a breath, fighting off the urge to break down then and there. Seeing her mother so upset and vulnerable, pouring out all her emotions to her, tore at her soul deep within. "I don't want to go," she whispered.

"What?"

"I don't want to go back, I'm not ready." Hannah pulled her knees to her chest as her eyes drifted away and across the yard to gather her thoughts. "I've been doing some thinking. I don't want to lose you."

"You won't."

"But Dad—"

Delilah grasped both her hands to jerk her attention back on her. Her eyes were peering into hers. "Hannah, you won't. I promise. Sweetie, you belong in New York. I am so proud of you. You are going to go so far in this life." A gentle squeeze nudged her on. "Your father would be proud as well. A few months, and you can come back here to visit."

Distrustfully, Hannah lowered her eyes away as her mood darkened. Another fear pawed at the door to her mind. Would the distance separate her and Jimmy for good? Her previous relationship with Greg fizzled after she decided to go to Ohio with her mother for a while. Other circumstances doused that fire, but the concept was the same. Jimmy was private and never openly disclosed any past relationships or other interests. Seeing the trouble stirring in her daughter, Delilah called to her gently, "What is it, honey?"

"What about Jimmy?" Hannah questioned. "What if I go to New York, then lose him?"

"You are young, Hannah—"

"I love him."

"I know."

"He could easily find someone else."

"Hannah, have you spoken with him?"

"He told me that he would wait for me."

"Then you have to believe him. I know losing Greg was hard on you, but you have to trust him." A playful smirk appeared on the woman's face. "Besides, this is a small, close-knit town, and people talk. I got tabs on him and will keep him straight." This aroused a giggle of approved amusement from Hannah.

"That, no doubt."

Looking down at her dirty clothes, Delilah stretched out. "I need a shower. Let's wash off and grab some lunch." Just as she moved to the doorway, she paused and spun around on her heel to look back at her daughter who was still sitting down. "You coming, Attorney Marks?"

Hannah's eyes lit up hearing the forespoken professional title, and she beamed as she stood up. "Yes, Ma'am."

August 11

The sunlight piercing the pulled thin curtains stirred Hannah that morning from her slumber. Feeling the caress of her bare skin touching the sheets, she turned slightly to look over her shoulder to see Jimmy's backside to her on his side of his bed where he slept. The drawn-back sheets were tantalizing, revealing his naked form just down to his upper part of his buttock. Chewing her lip as images flashed back into her mind from the night before made her grin giddily as she turned around to snatch her cellphone on the nightstand. With a quick unlock and a few maneuvers with her fingers, she pulled up her email to locate the flagged email that contained her boarding pass for her departure from Dayton later that afternoon. The destination: "LAG." The flight details provided gate information and time of departure, estimated arrival, and verification of the trip being one way. A lump formed in her throat as her eyes froze on that piece. Sighing, she pressed her head against the pillow and stared up at the ceiling before lowering her sight back onto Jimmy. Fate could have her leave Ohio this time for good. No weekend excursion, and back to life as usual. She would be gone for months, and with her internship spanning into the spring semester, she could have to stay in the Big Apple for a longer duration than anticipated. Where would that leave her? Her bond with her mother was solid, and it wasn't like her mother couldn't visit. They tore down the old foundation and patched what holes were there. She felt solid. Jimmy was a whole other issue.

Uncertainty gripped her, and like a lost child, she slid over behind him and wrapped her hands around his waistline, pulling him closer—an unspoken request of affirmation. Groaning softly as he came to, he looked back at her tiredly with a big yawn. "Hey, hon."

"Hey, yourself." She happily nuzzled his face and unloosed her arms as she felt him turning to face her.

Flipping onto his back, he reached out with his other arm and drew her close as his lips gently pressed against hers. "You been up long?"

"Nope."

Nodding his head, he traced her spine daintily with his fingertips, sending chills up her body. "You excited for your big day?" She anticipated his question, and yet she had no words to come to her. Her hesitation made him follow up, "You all right, sweetie?"

"Yeah, just... overwhelmed." She laughed a little, trying to play off her ever-growing anxiety. "I can't believe I got all my packing done!"

"You are going to be amazing. I'm proud of you." He leaned his head down and gently took in her lips again.

Wanting to end the discussion, she pressed her lips deeper into his, flicking the tip of her tongue over his teasingly as she held onto his left shoulder. His moan caught her off guard as he cupped her face, capturing her lips more heatedly as his body rolled on top of hers. She yearned for him. She wanted to stay in this moment forever.

Before proceeding with what would happen next soon, Jimmy surprisingly broke the kiss and caressed his skin. "We promised your mother we would meet for breakfast before heading to Dayton."

"We have time." Hannah leaned up and lightly kissed his neck in hopes of enticing him to cease further discussion. A part of her silently hoped that they would get so lost in one another that she would miss her flight. Though another could be rescheduled. Still, she needed one more day.

"Damn," he chuckled as he allowed her to continue her efforts. "You keep on, and I may just keep you here."

Hannah grinned at him. "So?"

"Now, now." Jimmy scooted off her and sat on the bed, pulling the sheet over his lower waist to hide his body's natural reaction to her kisses. "I will feel awful if I make you miss your flight."

"You can make it up to me," she cooed into his ear as she relentlessly pursued him and wrapped her arms around his neck loosely, with a quick kiss on his cheek.

He warmly smiled at her. "I'm going to miss you."

"Me too, Jimmy." She frowned as tears hit her face. She was unable to hold to her boiling emotions anymore. "I don't want to lose this."

"You won't…" He took his finger and gingerly wiped a few of the tears away. "I promise."

This vow didn't quench her fear. Her eyes were longing for more reassurance. "My last long-distance relationship didn't work out so well." Sparing him the details of what transpired between her and Greg following her father's death and her departure from the city.

"I'm not like him," Jimmy pressed on as he took her hand in his, squeezing it. "I will make sure that I won't lose you."

"I love you." The only three words that she could get out of her mouth from his response—the important ones.

"And I love you, Hannah Marks." He softly kissed her lips. After several seconds of silence, he glanced at his watch. "You know what? We have two hours before breakfast. You woke me up early."

"Okay." Hannah missed the mark as she nodded his head to his statement.

Growling playfully, he pushed her back down on the bed. "We have time!"

With her carry-on luggage pulled along behind her, Hannah paused just past the terminal entrance to swipe through her phone to grab the barcode details to check in at the kiosk. She felt rushed as she desperately looked over her shoulder to see Jimmy approaching her with her two check-in bags, and her mother standing off to the side to allow her to check in. He set the bags down as they waited for her to turn to scan before heading to the counter. After a few keystrokes, when it was her turn, she was able to get the labels printed out to place around the luggage straps, with her boarding details and her arrival destination. "LAG." The big pronounced, bold letters reminding her of where she was going and the fact that it was another change in her life that she would have to adapt to in a little over a year. Jimmy assisted her in getting the bags properly tagged before carrying them over to the security guard. The TSA member was a robust woman in her midforties with chopped-off hair and piercing, judging blue eyes. She remained silent as she motioned with her hand to direct Jimmy on placing the bags on the counter to allow her accomplice to check them. Hannah knew she didn't bring any contraband with her, but just the woman's icy stare made her feel guilty. How did Jimmy stay so calm? The woman glanced over Hannah's boarding pass before handing it back to her. "Thank you, ma'am." Her response was unexpected and soft. Quite the opposite of the exterior shell that she presented to passengers.

Bewildered, Hannah fumbled to pick up her carry-on to walk to her mom so the trio could make their way up the escalator to the upper floor, where the gates were. The airport was a bit more bustling than she remembered from her arrival, though it didn't compare at all to the crowds that La Guardia worked with daily. The logistics had to be so complex there. Their walk to her designated gate and security was silent despite the ambient chatter of other passengers in their conversations as they passed by. They were early, but Hannah felt so rushed. It was as if an unknown force was controlling her. She wanted to slow her steps down, to almost crawl. She continued to move about. With each foot press, her heartbeat went faster. She didn't want to leave. Not now. Where did the time go? Time felt so short and almost stolen from her. It was practically months ago when she arrived here with her mother. She was cold, filled with disdain. She wanted nothing to do with Delilah, and Jimmy didn't even exist in her life. She vowed to return to New York as quickly as possible. Yet here she was. About to debark on her adventure, and her feet were growing cold. She wanted to continue to be part of her mother's life, and she still wanted Jimmy's existence to remain intact. As if on cue, her boyfriend quickened his pace to match hers and squeezed her hand. "Eager?" He smiled encouragingly.

Hannah noticed the security station straight ahead, and that threw her off from responding right away. The point of no return. With the changes in airport security, those without boarding passes could not go past security. That meant Jimmy and Delilah could not go where she went after that. They were about thirty minutes early before her departure, and her plane was already at its spot to be loaded. The line to get through security was not long at all despite the airport's crowd. She had to wait ten minutes tops so far. She had time more than enough time to spend extra minutes with her mom and Jimmy for their farewells. "This is it." Delilah sniffed through choked tears as her glossy eyes looked at her daughter. Her face was filled with pride and joy. Everything that the pair went through, they endured and grew so much stronger through it all. The challenges that Delilah and Hannah made together were those alone. No one could take credit for it. "I am so proud of you, sweetie." She moved in and embraced her daughter tightly as she was unable to hold back the tears of sorrow and joy. Her sniffles broke down Hannah's strong will, and she cried along with her as they hugged. "You are going to go far, I know it," Delilah whispered to her through her hair.

Hannah tightened her embrace as she could smell her mother's recognizable cherry blossom fragrance. "Thank you, Mom… for everything. I am going to miss you."

"You will be fine, sweetie." Delilah stepped back to wipe her eyes. "You can call me anytime, you know that, and you are welcome back here. I love you."

Hannah smiled as big as she could. "I love you too."

Jimmy finally stepped into their private conversation after giving them time to say their farewells. "Knock them dead, girl. You got this." He moved in and sweetly kissed her lips, then pushed his head to her left ear and whispered, "I will be waiting for you."

"Thanks." Hannah took a deep breath and straightened her shoulders as if she tried to regain her composure to save face. "I love you, Jimmy. Stay out of trouble."

"You know I will keep tabs on him. Small town." Her mother smirked as she nudged Jimmy playfully in the side.

"Probably would." He laughed.

Nodding her head, Hannah took another breath and spun on her heel to head to security. At the cusp of the line entrance, she recoiled from her intention and hurried back to where Jimmy was still standing. His look of confusion was met with her passionate and fiery kiss that nearly knocked him off his feet. He lifted her as he returned the kiss and spun her around as he held her in his arms. "Baby girl, it will be all right. You are not losing me." He nestled her forehead with his as his eyes stared right into her own.

Biting her lip, tears flooded down her face. She ignored the perplexed look of passersby, who happened to be at the right moment to witness the romantic exchange. His words felt like they were not enough to quench her anxiety. Her heart ached terribly. She never felt this roller coaster of emotions before and never thought such a feeling was possible. Her body shook as she tried to persevere through it all. "I don't want to leave you."

"Just a few months, and I promise I will visit next month for a weekend once you get settled in." He kissed her again soothingly. "You can show me around."

She laughed at the afterthought, and his proposal did produce tranquility for her. "I'll hold you to that."

"You are going to miss your flight," he urged her as he motioned toward her destined direction with his head.

"I'm going, I'm going." She laughed as she kissed him again, then moved away from him.

"Come here." Jimmy grabbed her hand after she took two steps and pulled her close. His mouth was capturing hers once more.

"Come on, you two," Delilah cackled as she remained where she was, trying her best not to look, especially at her daughter in a public display of intense passion with a man. "You are making me feel awkward."

Picking up her luggage arm once more, Hannah forced herself to move on and get in line, not looking back. Her face was still warm from their goodbye, and she flushed at the guard who was standing at his post and most likely saw the whole thing go down. Avoiding direct eye contact, Hannah waited for her turn to pass through the metal detector and await her items to come through the x-ray scan. The way the security line turned, she could no longer see her mom or Jimmy at the entrance. Feeling her heart grow heavy, she exhaled sadly, then pressed on with her bag in tow to find her gate. The next stop was New York. As she progressed, she beamed with pride at her accomplishments. She felt like a whole new person since she left the large island after the holidays. A sense of new maturity overcame her. God threw her a curveball. She still didn't understand his reasoning behind taking her father at such a young age, and she may never have come to terms with it. Perhaps she didn't have that spiritual understanding of the higher power calling like a clergy member. Things happen for a reason, and in the end, it meant her father's ultimate sacrifice to bridge the gap between her and her mother, and perhaps even go as far as putting Jimmy in her life. A man that she never thought would have existed. Staring out the window at her plane, her mind continued to travel down the winding path, unlocking each door as it went to reveal more revelations. Flashbacks of brief moments of her life in Ohio. The good and the bad. Now here she was, waiting to board her plane. A slight smile spread across her glossy mauve lips. "Just like you always told me, Dad. I had to adapt to change. I hope whatever I do in my life that you are here with me, seeing it all." She giggled at a private thought as she continued the soft-spoken words, "And approve of Jimmy."

The announcement of her section of the plane being boarded awakened her from her words, and she broke away from the window to head into the queue that was already forming. Her printed boarding pass was held tightly in her hand, with her other pulling along her luggage. When it was her turn, she handed the attendant her pass and then strolled ahead through the docking tunnel. She could hear the multiple footsteps of those in front of her and behind her, eager to take their seats. Hannah took another breath. "Here goes nothing."

Epilogue

January 25, the Following Year

Her solace inside one of the study rooms at the Elmer Holmes Bobst Library that afternoon provided profuse silence and privacy that she needed to immerse herself in her preparation for the upcoming mock civil trial. The small room offered no windows and a windowless door. The walls were painted with a plain white color, and the chairs were wooden and supportless for one's back after countless hours of sitting. She wiggled her hips from side to side in the chair's divot as she tried to get a bit more comfortable. Staying off campus was a complete joy, and having Beth as a roommate was great. The two got along fine, and she didn't have to worry about the horror stories as one may often hear about college campus living drama. Despite the luck in her off-campus living, she often retreated to the library. The studio apartment offered little to no privacy, so it was hard to get off one another's schedule to study alone. Since they were both tenants, she couldn't simply ask Beth to leave and not come back for more than two hours. Fortunately for her that day, her afternoon was free, and she was able to secure a study room to hunker down and prep. The trial was coming up in three days. She would be defending a dog owner whose ten-pound cocker spaniel nipped the upper forearm of an eight-year-old girl who teased it. The bite was nothing and didn't break the skin. The child's parent did not alert the authorities nor take the child for any treatment that day but claimed following the incident that his daughter sustained hellish nightmares and flashbacks to where she would constantly cry without reason and refused to go outside in fear of seeing the dog again. The dog owner denied any responsibility and claims that the daughter trespassed on her property where the dog was leashed correctly, and agitated the dog with her friends. When she got too close, the dog had no choice but to defend itself.

Hannah rolled her eyes at the supposed transcript of the testimonies that she scrolled through on her tablet while she glanced over at the stack of books along with blown-up colored photos of the child's arm. There was a slight indentation of the dog's incisor on the skin, though no laceration or abrasion. Then her professor gave her the supposed medical records with the assignment—ten visits within three months to a psychologist. The diagnosis was post-traumatic stress disorder and anxiety. He recommended the ongoing need for monthly counseling for the next two years to help her estimate future costs up into the thousands. "Typical," she scoffed as she skimmed the transcript. It seemed like a case straight out of reality court shows.

Switching over to her laptop, she pulled up her search engine as she referred to a notebook to where she jotted down notes and keywords that stuck out. A wave of nausea hit her as she turned her head, and she paused with her fingertips hovering over the keyboard as she let it subside. Her stomach gurgled. Realizing it must have been hours since breakfast, she rummaged through her backpack in the seat next to her to locate the pack of peanut butter crackers that she stashed along with her. Inside her bag was also a note from Jimmy that he wrote her when she left Ohio following the winter holiday. She smiled as she pulled it out. Hannah already knew what he said; she must have read it at least five times since she got back. It wasn't lengthy at all but the reassurance of his devotion to her. A smile moved on her lips as she popped in a bite of the cracker, crunching along. Time moved so fast, and it just felt like a week ago when she came back to New York to see her mom and Jimmy. Christmas felt much different than it did last year. Nothing could fill the void left in her thoughts and heart from the loss of her father, Robert Marks.

Yet the newness of it all was uplifting. Inspiring. A stepping-stone for her path ahead.

Greg's absence made her return to New York easier. Even Beth didn't bring up his name. A part of her remained curious and desired to ask where he was and if he found anyone else. She remained steadfast against this. After all, this was a new chapter in her life. There was no going back.

After the winter break, everything felt rushed. She received two reminders of the importance of applying for internships ahead of time despite March's deadline. The push was not only from her multiple professors but even her guidance counselor. With her due diligence, she extended requests to several prestigious firms in Manhattan, including her father's. She was not the only one since every law student at her level was doing the same thing. The firms would go through each request, examine their credentials, then those that passed that part of the selection would be lined up for face-to-face interviews. The internship acceptance didn't freak her out like most. After all, her dad's company would instantly catch her name. Her request to them was just a formality and a reminder that she was still interested. All the documents were submitted two weeks ago, right when she returned to campus, to stay ahead of the game. Then there was complete silence. This stonewalled her. What if her absence from the school would go noticed? Indeed, her dad's company would understand this and overlook it.

As her mind bombarded with what-if gloom-and-doom scenarios, she abruptly paused and inhaled slowly through her nose, then exhaled. This kind of distraction was speculative, and she had to cease its existence. She had to remain regimented for this trial since its result and the subsequent mock trial in March weighed more than half of her final grade in the class. Crunching along with another bite of cracker in her mouth, she diverted her attention back to the photos that sprawled out on the table in the middle. The snack was causing acute nausea to subside. Her life schedule was in flux with all the pressures of her course load. She forgot dates such as her dental appointments, among other things, and it looked like eating was adding itself to the list.

The unexpected vibrational hum from her cell nearly made her jump out of her seat. Snatching it up to stop it pulsating against the wooden table, she read the display and recognized, first off, the caller to have an area code for the tristate area. It was pretty local to her. The familiarity of the number at first vexed her, then her eyes widened as she finally identified the caller. Her breath stopped as her fingers trembled along with the plastic case. This soon? She debated on answering the call or letting it just go to voice mail. Biting her lip, she quickly diverted her attention back to her work. This could be a life-changing event. She had to accept the call. Her mind would profusely deny her studies unless she knew right away. "Hello?" her voice timidly answered on the final ring.

"Yes, is this Ms. Hannah Marks?" a female replied on the other end.

She took another breath. "This is she." Her eyes closed as she awaited the news.

About the Author

Melinda Brown was born in Roanoke, Virginia. She has been writing as a hobby since she was a teenager. Special requests from her friends are a challenge for her, and Melinda savors every minute of it. She is a graduate of Roanoke College, with a major in history and a minor in education. She loved the short film screenwriting class that she took at Hollins University as part of their graduate program.

In her earlier years, she loved traveling to New York City yearly. Now she enjoys adventures with her husband and daughter.